W9-BSL-765

ALE

SERVICE DE LUXE
SAN FRANCISCO—LOS ANGELES—SAN DIEGO

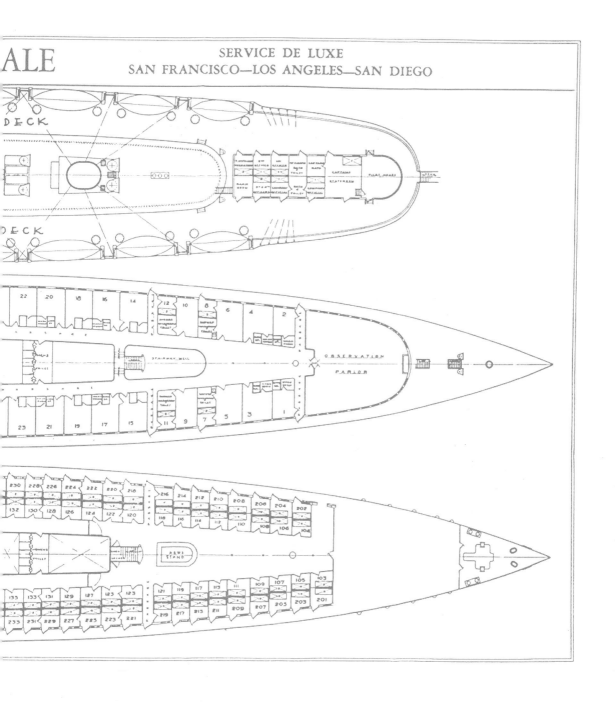

PACIFIC MARITIME HISTORY SERIES

Number 4

Published by the
ASSOCIATES OF THE NATIONAL MARITIME
MUSEUM LIBRARY

THE
WHITE FLYERS

The Harvard, *right, and* Yale *at a San Pedro, California, berth before World War I. Due to the overnight coastwise service they provided the two ships were seen together in the same port only for short periods of time. San Francisco Maritime National Historical Park Photographic Collection*

THE
WHITE FLYERS

HARVARD

AND

YALE

AMERICAN
COASTWISE TRAVEL

by
George F. Gruner

Associates of the National Maritime Museum Library
Pacific Maritime History Series

San Francisco
2002

Photo editor: Michael J. Mjelde
The illustration on the front cover is from the author's collection. The back cover illustrations are from the Bill Stritzel Collection and the author's collection.

Copyright © 2002 by
Associates of the National Maritime Museum Library

Published by Associates of the National Maritime Museum Library
at The Glencannon Press

The Glencannon Press
P.O. Box 341, Palo Alto, CA 94302
Tel. 800-711-8985
www.glencannon.com

First Edition, first printing.

Library of Congress Cataloging-in-Publication Data will be available on request from the publisher as soon as it is received.
"As a result of the events of September 11, 2001, the anthrax contamination on Capitol Hill, and the implementation of more stringent security measures, the Cataloging in Publication Division of the Library of Congress reported delays in mail processing for both Cataloging in Publication (CIP) and Pre-assigned Control Number (PCN) processing." The Library of Congress

Dedication

For Irene — Her turn

ACKNOWLEDGEMENTS

It is not unusual for a ship historian to owe much to the library staffs of maritime museums wherever those ships sailed. What is out of the ordinary is the record trail on this project, which leads far inland. But the bulk of the information, and the photographs, came from these individuals and their institutions, so heartfelt thanks go to them first:

Irene Stachura, librarian, and Bill Kooiman, technician, J. Porter Shaw Library, San Francisco Maritime National Historical Park; Ann C. House, librarian, Steamship Historical Society of America Collection, University of Baltimore Library; F. Michael Angelo, former library director, Independence Seaport Museum, Philadelphia; Jean Beckner, Special Collections librarian, Honnold/Mudd Library, Claremont-McKenna College, Claremont, California, and Alan Jutzi, Avery chief curator, rare books, The Huntington Library, San Marino.

Much valuable assistance was supplied by John L. Whitmeyer, historian associated with the Los Angeles Maritime Museum, San Pedro; Robert C. Niles, research associate at the Maine Maritime Museum, Bath; Myra M. Manfrina, director of the Lompoc Valley Historical Society; Eric Gillespie, associate director of the Col. Robert R. McCormick Research Center, Cantigny First Division Museum, Wheaton, Illinois; Kathleen Plourd, Collections Services, Chicago Historical Society; John C. Reilly, Jr., Operational Archives Branch, Naval Historical Center, Washington Navy Yard; Susan Hengel, Imprints Department, Hagley Museum and Library, Wilmington, Delaware.

Also Diane Kaplan, archivist, Yale University; Pam Harper, Delaware County Historical Society, Broomall, Pennsylvania; Brian A. Sullivan, reference archivist, Harvard University; Richard Peuser, archivist, National Archives II, College Park, Maryland; Robert P. Molander, my Fresno editor; the late George Belyea, ocean sailboater and supplier of navigational data; Captain Walter Jaffee of The Glencannon Press, for his advocacy and production skills; Pete Evans, Richard Geiger and John Kortum of the Associates of the National Maritime Museum Library Publication Committee for their support; Bill Stritzel for his artifacts; my wife, Irene Lee Gruner, a full partner in every phase of this work, and the staffs of the San Diego Historical Society, the San Diego Maritime Museum, the Henry Madden Library, California State University, Fresno, and the Fresno County Public Library.

I cannot forget Ken Hohman of Fresno, who, on hearing me tell of this project, produced a mint-perfect copy of a *Harvard* three-fold illustrated mailer dated Oct. 8, 1926 — he had retrieved it from a Los Angeles garage attic some years before. Its illustration graces the cover to remind me that when it comes to historical research, facts — or artifacts — are where you find them.

— G.F.G.

Contents

PROLOGUE

From the time their hulls hit the water to almost the very end of their dramatic lives, the sister coastal passenger ships *Yale* and *Harvard* rarely were mentioned without accompanying adjectives denoting speed, luxury and grace.

Designed in Scotland and built in 1906-07 in two American yards, they were harbingers of an era then dawning in world maritime affairs. They were called the "White Flyers" and the "palatial super-express steamships," and the "crack freight and passenger carriers." But it was the method of propulsion that set them apart. In the first wave of turbine-powered steamships in the United States — and the biggest yet built in America — the triple-screw *Yale* and *Harvard* most frequently were labeled "the fast turbiners," capable of regular service at average speeds of more than 20 knots. Also pioneers in the fuel switchover from coal to oil, they gained distinction through sustained service on both Atlantic and Pacific Coasts and with the U.S. Navy in the English Channel in World War I. *Yale* rejoined the fleet in World War II, long after *Harvard* broke up on a rocky California shore, taking her place on the list of great shipwrecks of the Pacific Coast.

The fast turbiners have been only memories for more than half a century, yet they share a chapter in American maritime history — not giant transatlantic carriers or glamorous cruise liners, but coastal speedsters that transported thousands of passengers between major ports on both eastern and western seaboards.

Their story is worth a detailed telling.

THE
WHITE FLYERS

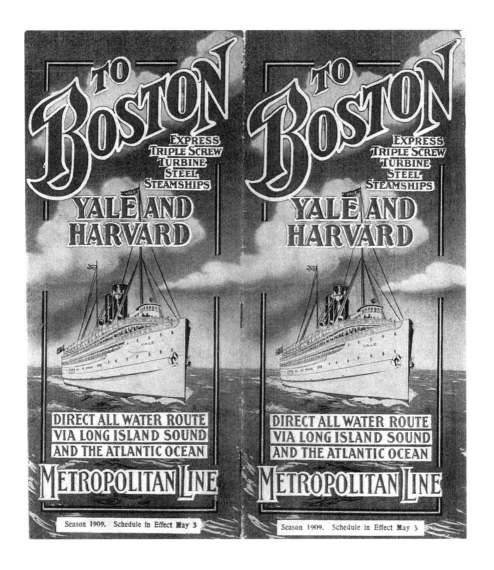

PART I

THE SHIPS

4 THE WHITE FLYERS

1

CHARLIE PARSONS' MARINE TURBINE

At the dawn of the twentieth century, steam had replaced sail as the source of power in the world's great maritime fleets. Ocean-going vessels and mighty naval units relied on the force of high-pressure steam reacting on pistons, moving ponderously up and down in giant cylinders, to operate gears and turn propeller shafts. And on the coasts, lakes and rivers, the era of the paddlewheel steamer was on the wane, as more shipbuilders turned to the screw propeller even as a newer form of motive power appeared.

Charles A. Parsons, engineer son of a British earl and long involved in propulsion development, conceived the marine turbine, in which high-pressure jets of steam spun rows of multibladed fans to turn a ship's propeller at speeds never previously attained. He unveiled his new power plant to the world at Spithead, England, in June, 1897, before a multinational fleet assembled for a naval review honoring Queen Victoria's Diamond Jubilee.

Parsons' demonstration vessel was the forty-two-ton *Turbinia*, which developed 2,400 horsepower. Evading patrol craft guarding the naval review site, *Turbinia* raced down the line of anchored ships at speeds up to 34.5 knots, confounding captains and admirals while proving turbine power could and would ride the waves of the future.

Despite her unassuming appearance, the Turbinia *changed marine propulsion forever when she galloped through an assembled international fleet at the 1897 Naval Review at Spithead, England, leaving conventional steam launches trying to catch her far astern in her wake.* The Encyclopedia Of Ships

Within a few years, British Adm. Jackie Fisher, father of the prototype battleship *Dreadnought*, chose turbines to power that landmark vessel. Almost simultaneously, directors of the Cunard Line, after competitive tests between reciprocating and turbine engines in smaller vessels, decided on turbine power for its great new liners, the 31,938-ton *Lusitania* and *Mauretania*. All three ships were launched in 1906, just as Parsons developed ties to American companies to build turbines based on his patents.

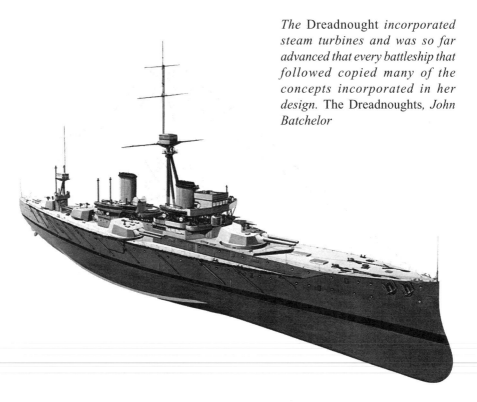

The Dreadnought *incorporated steam turbines and was so far advanced that every battleship that followed copied many of the concepts incorporated in her design.* The Dreadnoughts, *John Batchelor*

Left to right are the Mauretania*'s astern, low-pressure ahead and high-pressure ahead turbines. The workers in the photo give a sense of scale. The* Yale *and* Harvard *turbines would have been similar, although smaller.* Engineering

The Lusitania *in the port of Liverpool before one of her transatlantic runs. A German torpedo ended her career in May, 1915.* Ocean Liners

The *Lusitania*, on her record-breaking maiden voyage, averaged speeds better than 25 knots, arriving in New York on Sept. 13, 1907 after four-and-a-half days, three days before *Yale* and *Harvard* began regular New York-to-Boston service. The *Lusitania*'s life was cut short by a torpedo from a German submarine on May 7, 1915, but the *Mauretania* held the transatlantic record for twenty years, eventually achieving a top average speed of 26.20 knots. Even before Cunard ships entered the competition for the Blue Riband, symbol of the Atlantic speed record, the reputation of Parsons' Marine Steam Turbine Company reached the United States and set heads and wheels spinning.

Charles Wyman Morse was responsible for the first American-flag steam turbine-powered ship. The Steamship Historical Society of America Collection, Langsdale Library, University of Baltimore

The Governor Cobb *was the first turbine-powered vessel in the United States. She was built in 1906 and replaced the* St. Croix *on the International Line serving Canadian ports. Marine Museum of Fall River, Massachusetts*

Into waters long dominated by the paddlewheel-driven vessels of the Hudson River, Long Island Sound, Chesapeake Bay and the Great Lakes stepped a new player ready to get his feet wet — Charles W. Morse. His aces in the contest with J. Pierpont Morgan and other maritime magnates of the day were to be his fast turbiners, the *Yale* and the *Harvard*. Morse tested the new propulsion system in a smaller vessel built at the John Roach shipyard near Philadelphia for his Eastern Steamship Company, the 2,522-ton freighter *Governor Cobb* (Maine Gov. William Cobb just happened to be an Eastern director). She was the first turbine-powered ship to fly the American Flag.

Launched on April 21, 1906, the *Governor Cobb* was moved to the W. & A. Fletcher yard in Hoboken, New Jersey, where her engines were built and installed. She made her first trial run on the Hudson River on Oct. 17, hitting 17.5 knots, and on Nov. 1 made her first run up the East River, through Long Island Sound and around Cape Cod to Boston at an average speed of 18 knots, quickly establishing the ascendancy of turbines over pistons in practical, everyday use.

Morse (who had ordered a second triple-screw turbiner, the 2,153-ton *Camden* to be built at the Bath Iron Works for his Bangor Line) gave the go-ahead for the *Yale* and *Harvard*. Charlie Parsons' great invention would make Morse's dreams of a new shipping empire come true.

The Camden *as she appeared in 1907. The second turbine-powered vessel to fly the American Flag, she served in C.W. Morse's Bangor Line. Steamship Historical Society of America (From the Collection of Frank E. Claes).*

2

THE SHIPS

Except for the interior décor, determined by their individual names and the universities they honored, the *Yale* and the *Harvard* were almost identical down to the last nut and bolt. Observed in misty weather, their dual raked stacks billowing clouds of black smoke and their sleek white hulls churning up trails of froth as they surged past plodding freighters, lumber schooners and fishing vessels, it was impossible to tell them apart without reference to their posted schedule. But then it was easy — observers could set their watches as the fast turbiners traveled their scheduled routes like clockwork. At first it was between New York and Boston, then San Francisco and Los Angeles/San Diego. For a time, it was even Southampton and Le Havre/Brest.

The ships' names stemmed from the fact that entrepreneur Charles W. Morse had a son attending each school (Morse also commissioned a *Princeton* for his Hudson River route, but that was another ship and another story). As originally designed for the New York-Boston run, both the *Yale* and the *Harvard* were licensed to carry 1,000 passengers but each actually contained 987 berths in 311 staterooms — forty of them deluxe suites with parlors and thirty with private bathrooms ("more than any coastwise ship or palatial steamer in this country" was the claim).

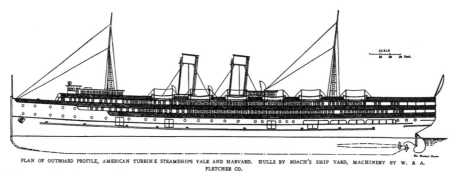

PLAN OF OUTBOARD PROFILE, AMERICAN TURBINE STEAMSHIPS YALE AND HARVARD. HULLS BY ROACH'S SHIP YARD, MACHINERY BY W. & A. FLETCHER CO.

This profile plan was featured in The Nautical Gazette *as part of the article describing the two ships. The sleek vessels were over 400 feet long.*

Based on ship plans drawn in Dumbarton, Scotland, by William Denny and Bros. to meet international maritime regulations, the two ships cost $1,225,000 each, a not insignificant sum when one considers the vessels were expected to operate in the four- or five-month summer season and lay up during the winter (although it was hoped some winter charters could be arranged). When completed early in 1907 their statistics were:

Length over all:	407 feet, four inches.
Length between perpendiculars:	386 feet, six inches.
Breadth, molded:	50 feet, six inches.
Breadth, over guards:	63 feet.
Draft, loaded:	16 feet.
Gross tonnage:	3,731.
Net tonnage:	2,312.
Horsepower:	12,000.

The hulls were built in the yard of the Delaware River Iron Ship-building & Engine Works, known as the John Roach Shipyard, in Chester, Pennsylvania, a suburb of Philadelphia. Roach was a pioneer in the development of steel vessels and in 1894 produced the "ABCD ships" (USS *Atlanta,* USS *Boston,* USS *Chicago* and USS *Dolphin*), the first units of America's proclaimed "New Navy," in which steel hulls would replace antiquated ships of iron and wood. The Roach yard also built many of the steamships operated in the coastal trade as well as ocean steamers sailing the Pacific and the Atlantic.

After their launch in December, 1906, and January, 1907, the *Yale* and *Harvard* hulls were towed by tugs down Chesapeake Bay and up to New York harbor to the works of W. & A. Fletcher Company of Hoboken, New Jersey, where the machinery was built and installed. As with the

The steamers Yale *and* Harvard *being outfitted at the wharves of the W. & A. Fletcher Co. of Hoboken, New Jersey where their power plants were built.* The Nautical Gazette

Governor Cobb, deckhouses and joiner work were completed by John Englis & Son of Greenpoint, Brooklyn.

The Fletcher yard did not undertake the pioneering work blindly. Andrew Fletcher, the company president, and Calvin Austin, head of Morse's Eastern Line, had traveled to Britain to study the new turbine engines. Fletcher spent several months at the Parsons plant and made trips on European turbine vessels to become expert in their operation.

Each ship was of steel double-hull construction, divided by bulkheads into watertight compartments. Steam was produced in twelve three-furnace Scotch boilers in two fore-and-aft forced-draft firerooms separated by a bulkhead. As originally built, the ships burned coal, but conversion to oil came three years later. Each ship's three turbines were installed under license from the Parsons Marine Steam Turbine Company of Wallsend-on-Tyne, England, and New York City.

The high-pressure turbine was installed on the center line, with a low-pressure and astern turbine on each side. Each turbine drove a shaft and three-bladed bronze propeller, designated port, center and starboard. The starboard and center propellers were right-hand screws and the port left-hand. When the ships were traveling ahead, steam was directed at 155 pounds pressure through the center high-pressure turbine, then via exhaust to the forward ends of the port and starboard turbines and finally on to the condensers in the ships' wings. The astern turbines were built within the low-pressure port and starboard units. To stop the ships, or to maneuver, steam was cut off from the center turbine and directed to the left and right wheels, going astern together to stop or reversing on one and powering ahead on the other to produce a quick turn. To provide a large safety margin against complete loss of motive power, the engineering compartments were equipped with two sets of condensers, circulating air systems, water feed and oil pumps, and ample piping.

The ships' electrical systems, installed by the Western Electric Company, consisted of 1,600 lights, plus a General Electric twenty-four-inch searchlight, with inside electric controls. Electric call bells in each room were fitted with thermostatic pushbuttons connected to an annunciator system which would enable officers in any part of the ship to determine the location of a fire should one break out. The ships carried the DeForest system of wireless telegraphy.

The *Nautical Gazette*, a contemporary trade publication, provided the most detailed picture of the *Yale*'s interior and exterior features shortly after the ship began regular service (the descriptions would apply equally to the *Harvard*, except the blue décor would be replaced with red materials):

The grand stairway of the main passenger saloon on the steamer Yale *exemplified seafaring opulence at the beginning of the twentieth century.* The Nautical Gazette

The top of the grand stairway as viewed from the gallery deck. The Nautical Gazette

The forward end of the Grand Saloon as it appeared in August, 1907. The Nautical Gazette

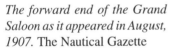

"To a trained nautical eye the *Yale* is perfection in her way, notwithstanding the large amount of superstructure, and has been pronounced the most graceful passenger steamship on our coasts. On her passages through the harbors and up and down the coast she never fails to elicit exclamations of admiration from landsman and sailor alike …

"Upon entering the quarter deck the passenger finds himself in a commodious and handsomely furnished social hall, finished entirely in mahogany. The deck is covered with interlocking tinted rubber tile … The staircase from the social hall to the upper saloons is one of the most attractive ever placed on an American vessel. Instead of a straight overhead ceiling under the stairs of the second deck, a circular half dome of pleasing design has been worked into the deck above … At the apex of this dome is carved a cherub's head, and with the letter Y incorporated in the design, is brilliant in gold leaf.

This view of the Grand Saloon shows part of the gallery and saloon decks and what was termed the "elaborate scheme of wall and ceiling decoration." The Nautical Gazette

"Electric globes light up the dome and stairway ... The side walls of the social hall are of mahogany and have neat hand-carved ornaments in the style of the Empire period ... The social hall has numerous easy armchairs of mahogany, upholstered in leather.

"The dining room is located on the main deck ... The massive doors at the entrance are of solid mahogany, with heavy plate glass extending nearly to the floor. The dining room is built of mahogany, with paneled ceiling, beautifully tinted in cream and verde gold. There are large windows on either side, placed in pairs, with elaborately ornamented panels between. Each set of windows has its individual lambrequin, in Yale blue, with gold braid trimmings ... Over the windows is a frieze of specially designed sea shells, etc., in gold and green. The ceiling is paneled in squares, to which ornaments in keeping with the general scheme of decoration are affixed, the electric light clusters emerging from the mouths of dolphins. On each table is an electrolier of stained glass in form of a seashell, with the letter Y on each, and held above a bronze crab as

The dining room of the steamer Yale. *The caption on this photo pointed out it was a "time photograph" taken while the vessel was running at twenty-four knots.* The Nautical Gazette

Among the areas set aside for passenger comfort were a smoking room and the writing room, right. The Nautical Gazette

the base. The tables, chairs, serving tables, buffets, etc., are of mahogany. The service is of specially made silver, and with the china and napery, bears the name of the Metropolitan Line.

"Ascending the stairs from the social hall the passenger enters the grand saloon, and as this is where the majority of the passengers pass the time, is of course the showplace of the vessel. Part of the main saloon, both forward and aft of the boiler enclosure, extends to the dome deck, there being galleries around the second saloon deck reached by an elaborate staircase in solid mahogany.

"In the matter of interior decoration and fittings the *Yale* strikes a new note, and it safe to say that in no American steamer yet built has there been so elaborate and beautiful a scheme of embellishment incorporated in the design. Yale blue is the color used wherever practicable, such as in the carpeting and upholstery, but the woodwork and ceilings of the upper cabins, of white enamel, give a feeling of cleanliness and brightness to the cabins which is missing on vessels finished in dark wood …

Accommodations included rooms in several price ranges. This is one of the deluxe staterooms. The Nautical Gazette

The mid-price stateroom included bunk beds and wood paneling, plus a primitive wash basin. Note the Metropolitan Line's emblem on the blanket in the lower bunk. Los Angeles Maritime Museum, collection of John L. Whitmeyer

"Ornaments especially designed for the *Yale* and *Harvard* are unique and are bewildering in their variety and beauty ... The most elaborate of these surmount the mainmast in the grand saloon aft, and consist of an arrangement of shells, dolphins, sea horses, lobsters, crabs and other members of the crustacean family, cleverly worked out and arranged in harmonious design most interesting and effective ...

"The decks of the saloon and galleries are laid with heavy Royal Wilton carpets, all specially made for the vessel, the wool being dyed Yale blue, in three shadings, in a handsome floral design. The upholstery of all chairs, sofas, etc. is of Yale blue figured plush, in perfect keeping with the carpeting ... All electric light brackets, doorknobs, escutcheons, and ... all hardware were specially designed for the vessel and have the verde antique effect.

"The smoking room is on the upper deck, aft of the smoke stacks, and is reached from the gallery deck. It is finished in Flemish oak, with a Dutch frieze showing barges, canals and the windmills familiar to Holland. There are a dozen circular tables in the room, with large armchairs, all of the same material as the trim of the room … The bar, which directly adjoins the smoking room, is elaborately fitted up, being finished in a style similar to the other apartment, and containing every necessary accessory, including large ice chest, cigar case, etc., etc …

"Keeping pace with the times, the galley and pantry outfit on these boats is arranged for strictly a la carte service … The galley proper is located directly below the saloon deck, aft of the machinery space, and extends the full width of the ship, with wide stairways entering directly from the dining saloon above. Extending athwartship and against the bulkhead next to the machinery space is the steel cooking range and broilers, containing five fires, with large steel pot racks above and ventilating hood with ducts extending up through the ventilating shafts. Directly in front of the range and broilers is located the steam table, with porcelain dishes and silver plated covers, which keeps the food warm while in process of serving …

"As the service on these vessels will be strictly a la carte, the apparatus has been designed expressly for this purpose. There are automatic egg boiling machines, oyster stewing kettles, steam bain-maries and coffee and tea urns. In the pantry there are suitable pudding steamers, cup warmers, urns and large roomy refrigerators for keeping salads, ices, fruits, etc. The scullery is equipped with an electric dish washing machine having a capacity of 8,000 dishes per hour. The silver cleaning department is located directly under the stairway, where there is an electric outfit for renovating, cleaning and polishing silver, etc."

The *Nautical Gazette* writer declared Morse had given orders that his vessels were to be "the fastest, safest and most luxuriously fitted ships in the country." The writer's descriptions indicated Morse's orders were being followed to the letter. But operating such vessels could not be done on the cheap — costs for their first season were reported to total $4,000 a day. Laying-up expenses were not insignificant, either — for the two ships the total was more than $52,000 in 1908 and nearly $66,000 in 1909.

3

MELTDOWN OF THE ICEMAN FROM MAINE

On February 7, 1907, even before his pet ships *Yale* and *Harvard* were ready for service, shipping entrepreneur Charles Wyman Morse offered to buy the maritime assets of the New York, New Haven and Hartford Railroad for $20 million, far more than their apparent worth. It was an "in your face" move by Morse against transatlantic tycoon J. Pierpont Morgan and his allies, who through the New Haven, as the railroad was called, were well on their way to domination of ship and rail freight and passenger service between New York and Boston.

The offer was typical of Morse, who already had a reputation for devious moves and a willingness to boldly challenge other industrial and financial tycoons of the time. (He made the same maneuver in 1905, offering Metropolitan Line President H.M. Whitney $3 million for his company, nearly three times more than it was worth. Whitney quickly took the deal.)

Morse's latest offer ultimately was rejected by the New Haven's board of directors, controlled by Morgan — the financial giant of the period did not suffer gladly those who dared threaten his operations. Even President Theodore Roosevelt weighed in on the side of the New Haven, giving the line a "green light" for expansion if it would just reject Morse's offer. The railroad pressed on with what already was its objective — defeating the upstart Morse and his johnny-come-lately ships about to steam at top speed over the competitive horizon.

But Morse was cast from the same mold as Morgan. From his beginnings he believed in fast-turning wheels and deals. Born in Bath, Maine, on Oct. 21, 1856, Morse had an immediate link to the sea — his grandfather and father controlled towing on the Kennebec River. Morse joined them while still attending Bowdoin College (Class of 1877), but avoided the tugboat wheelhouse in favor of the company office. Concentrating on the firm's assets, he gave an early showing of his penchant for financial manipulation and skill at turning the fast buck.

One of Bath's principal industries was the storing and shipping of winter ice for delivery to customers as far south as New Orleans (the average family icebox then consumed 2½ tons a year). Morse convinced his family a fortune was to be made in consolidating and owning the entire operation rather than just towing ice-laden schooners to their destinations. By 1899 his American Ice Company — one of the giant corporate trusts that became the target of Teddy Roosevelt's ire — monopolized deliveries to major east coast cities, giving Morse the title of "the Ice King".

The American Ice Company collapsed in 1900 (Morse's decision to double the New York prices from 25-30 cents to 60 cents per hundred pounds on one particularly hot day may have been a factor). Subsequently it was reported that New York's mayor and other Tammany Hall cohorts held stock in the company and had granted American Ice special privileges over its competitors. Morse by then wielded control through a holding company, Consolidated Ice, distributing 2½ million tons on 105 vessels. Morse escaped from the company's failure with a cool $12 million, enough to finance his moves into banking and shipping.

Morse began in 1901 by purchasing a steamboat line operating on the Kennebec River and between Bath and Boothbay Harbor. From that simple start in less than six years his Consolidated Steamship Company controlled many lines operating between Canada's Maritime Provinces and Galveston, earning Morse the new title of "Admiral of the Atlantic Coast." Such businesses as the Eastern Steamship Company, the Clyde Line, the Ward Line, the Mallory Line, Hudson Navigation Company (Albany night boat), the New York and Cuba Steamship Company and the New York and Puerto Rico Steamship Company became part of his operations, as did the Metropolitan Line, under whose flag he chose to battle Morgan, the powerhouse of the overnight boats.

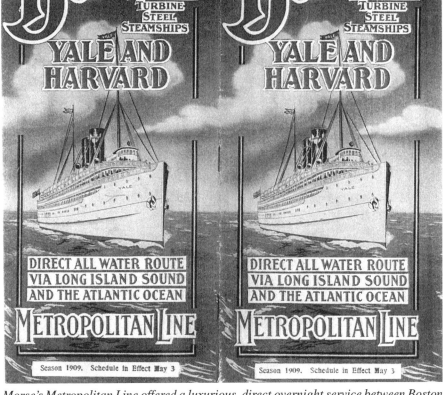

Morse's Metropolitan Line offered a luxurious, direct overnight service between Boston and New York City on a new "outside route." The Huntington Library

The competition was formidable — the New Haven had almost total control of freight and passenger traffic between New York and Boston. Its flagship steamboat operation was the Fall River Line, which carried overnight passengers from New York up Long Island Sound to Fall River, Massachusetts, where they transferred at 5:30 a.m. to express New Haven trains waiting at dockside to whisk them on to Boston for the start of the business day. The trip took twenty-two hours and required that passengers be rousted from their beds to make the pre-dawn boat-train transfer.

With delivery of his fast turbiners, Morse intended beating the New Haven by establishing the "outside route" — 337 miles up Long Island Sound into the Atlantic and around Cape Cod directly to Boston harbor, delivering passengers at 9 a.m. after a comfortable overnight passage of 14½ hours (direct service to Boston via a shorter route became possible for smaller, shallow-draft boats after the construction of the 7.7-mile Cape Cod Canal across the southwestern stretch of the cape, from Buzzards Bay to Cape Cod Bay, in 1909-14).

Just as the competing interests made major moves to bolster their forces in the impending battle for dominance on the northeast coast, the business recession of 1907

METROPOLITAN STEAMSHIP CO.
All-the-Way-by-Water

THE DIRECT ALL-THE-WAY-BY-WATER
PASSENGER SERVICE

OF THE METROPOLITAN LINE
Between
NEW YORK and BOSTON

will be operated during the Season of 1909, from Monday, May 3rd, to Saturday, October 30th, inclusive, during which period the fast Turbine Steel Steamships

YALE and HARVARD

will be in commission.

The Yale and Harvard are sister ships, each being 407 feet long and 63 feet in width, and were built especially for the route of the Metropolitan Line between New York and Boston. They are the fastest Merchant Vessels flying the American Flag.

They have sleeping accommodations for about 800 passengers; their appointments are most luxurious, while the service which they provide in every department appeals to the most fastidious.

SCHEDULE
Service Week Days and Sundays

From New York. Leave Pier 45, North River
(near foot of Christopher Street). at 5 P. M.
From Boston. Leave India Wharf at 5 P. M

Steamers are due to arrive at either end of the route at 8 o'clock the following morning.

The Run between the two cities is made in 15 hours, an average speed of 24 statute miles being maintained throughout the trip.

Opportunity is thus provided for an unbroken night's rest from City to City over the most fascinating Water Route in the World.

Service was seasonal, with the ships being laid up during the winter. Accommodations were promised to please even the most fastidious passenger. The Huntington Library

STEAMSHIP YALE: THE YALE AND HARVARD ARE SISTER SHIPS

The Metropolitan Line brochure included a photo of the Yale underway with bright white hull and black funnels. The Huntington Library

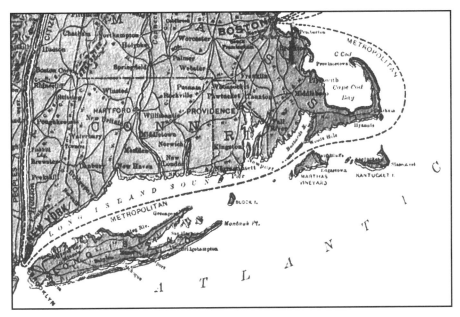

Morse's Metropolitan Line offered an all-water route that put the traveler in Boston or New York at the start of the business day, as opposed to Morgan's Fall River Line which required a train segment during the trip. The Huntington Library

created an unexpected run on two New York banks controlled by Morse. This precipitated the collapse of the Morse empire, which came even faster than his meteoric rise to the corporate heights.

The bank panic of October, 1907, caught Morse's financial resources overextended (at the time he owned ten banks and three insurance companies and held controlling stock in telephone, railroad and other interests worth more than $330 million). Stockholders took over most of his shipping lines in November and ultimately the majority of those companies were saved. On January 1, 1908, Consolidated Shipping missed an interest payment and on February 4 the company was placed in receivership. Metropolitan Line, heavily burdened by the costs of its great new ships, failed to pay its bills and creditors attached the two vessels.

Morse, meanwhile, was the central figure in an investigation of the failure of the National Bank of North America (the prosecuting district attorney was Henry L. Stimson, later to serve as secretary of war and secretary of state). By March Morse was formally charged with fraud in falsifying bank records and misuse of depositors' funds. He continued running his business interests while awaiting trial, which finally came before a federal court in October. On November 6 Morse was convicted and sentenced to fifteen years in a federal prison, but he filed an appeal and pending a hearing was confined in New York's Tombs Prison until

The Metropolitan Line had offices on India Wharf at Boston's Atlantic Avenue waterfront. Taken in 1906, this photo shows the H.M. Whitney *discharging into railcars on barges alongside while the coastal steamer* Prince George *heads for sea. Society for the Preservation of New England Antiquities*

released on bail in March, 1909. During his time in the Tombs, located only a few blocks from the Metropolitan Line pier, he was said to conduct business as usual from his jail cell.

Morse's appeal was heard in November, 1909, and his conviction and fifteen-year sentence were upheld. He was sent to the federal penitentiary in Atlanta in January, 1910. He then enlisted the services of Harry M. Daugherty (whose later career was tarnished by his role as President Warren G. Harding's attorney general during the Teapot Dome scandal) to seek a pardon from President William Howard Taft. Two panels of doctors examined Morse, who claimed to be dying. The first rejected the claim, but the second, composed of army doctors, said he suffered from Bright's disease and had only a few weeks to live if kept in custody. President Taft signed the pardon and Morse, released after serving little more than two years of his sentence, immediately went to Germany "for treatment." Daugherty failed to receive his promised fee and the government "learned" that Morse drank a combination of soapsuds and chemicals to produce the symptoms of Bright's disease noted by the second panel. President Taft claimed he was deluded, saying the whole Morse affair "shakes one's faith in expert examination."

Far from dying, Morse lived for an additional twenty-one years, returning to the United States and enduring other bouts with the law involving stock deals, allegations of investor fraud and failure to deliver on wartime government shipbuilding contracts. During his contentious career, however, he remembered his hometown, building a high school in 1903 and providing annual funds for its maintenance by registering some of his ships in Bath. Morse faced jail late in life, but his genuine weakened physical condition saved him. On September 7, 1926, he was placed under guardianship. He suffered several strokes and died of pneumonia in Bath on January 12, 1933.

During the leadership vacuum while Morse was occupied with banking woes, other owners were concerned about future prospects for *Yale* and *Harvard*, now facing takeover by creditors. Arcane corporate moves, some assisted or guided by the New Haven's lawyers, resulted in formation of two new Metropolitan Steamship Lines, one incorporated in New Jersey and the other in Maine. The ships were sold to the New Jersey firm and chartered to the Maine company to be operated by the latter during the 1910 season. Behind the scenes, efforts were underway to remove them from the east coast competitive picture.

Rumors that *Yale* and *Harvard* would be sold or chartered to Pacific Coast interests had circulated as early as their first season on the New York-Boston run (certainly it had been talked about in hopeful terms in the corridors of the New Haven's headquarters). The rumors were repeated in the spring of 1908 and again in October, 1909, when the Metropolitan Line's assets were sold to the Metropolitan Steamship Company of New Jersey.

In September, 1910, after more than two years of negotiations, the two ships were leased to the Pacific Navigation Company, incorporated in New Jersey but planning to remove the vessels from the Atlantic. Investigations in later years would reveal that the New Haven was the guiding force in shifting the White Flyers from the route they were designed to serve.

4

ATLANTIC DATEBOOK
I

December 24, 1906 —

Charles W. Morse's penchant for the flamboyant was evident in his plans for the first public event involving his two new "flyers," the launching and christening of the coastal turbiner *Yale*. How better to get the maximum attention in New York City, slated to be the southern terminus of the new overnight boats, than to take a trainload of folks to see his new vessel?

Morse did just that, ordering up a Pennsylvania Railroad eight-car special — four parlor cars, three dining cars and a smoker — to transport 150 guests the 210 miles south to Chester, Pennsylvania, direct to a siding in the John Roach Shipyard. The guest list was headed by Yale University President Arthur T. Hadley and his wife. Their seven-year-old daughter, Laura Beaumont Hadley, was to christen the ship. Other guests included representatives of various steamship lines, port officials and leaders of firms involved in the construction of the two ships, along with their wives and, in some cases, their children. (The event was staged under the direction of Orlando Taylor, former general passenger agent of the New Haven's New England Navigation Company, who had been lured away by Morse to a similar post with the Metropolitan Line.)

The Yale *as she appeared on the ways at Chester, Pennsylvania, five days before she was christened, with lightweight pole scaffolding along her side.* The Nautical Gazette

The starboard quarter of the Yale *as seen at Roach's yard just before launching in December of 1906. Note the absence of superstructure.* The Nautical Gazette

This view of the port quarter shows more of the flags in place for the launching ceremony. Note the group gathered on the pier. The Nautical Gazette

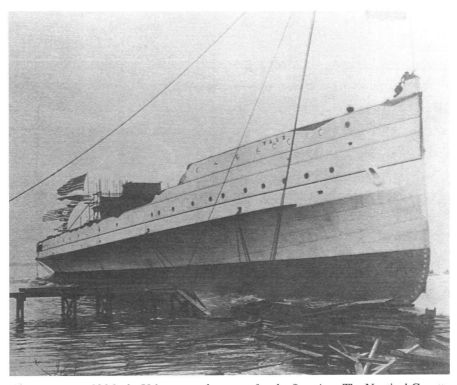

Christmas eve, 1906: the Yale *enters the water for the first time.* The Nautical Gazette

The blue of Old Yale was the dominant color on the invitations and in the decorations and the menu cards aboard the train — bouquets of violets were issued to the ladies and boutonnieres to the men. Each guest received a small Yale pennant, and even the boxes of fancy bonbons came in blue wrappers. A special gift to help her remember the occasion was reserved for the young Miss Hadley — a sapphire and diamond brooch.

Morse's special train left Jersey City at 9:15 a.m., arriving at Chester at noon. Switched directly to a yard siding, the guests were greeted by John H. Roach, president of the shipbuilding company. Roach led the christening party to the platform prepared at the *Yale*'s prow. The others gathered at vantage points in the crowd, which totaled about 3,000 spectators. Miss Hadley performed her duties and the launch, accompanied by cheers and the waving of hundreds of miniature Yale flags, went off without a hitch at 1 p.m., after which the guests returned to the train to partake of a gala luncheon en route back to New York.

February 1, 1907 —

Ceremonies marking the launch of the second of Morse's "new Boston boats" were a duplicate of what transpired with the *Yale*, except with the *Harvard* the predominant color was crimson and the guest list had a Bostonian caste. So experienced were the workers in John Roach's shipyard that the rites went off almost too smoothly — actually, fifteen minutes ahead of schedule.

Orlando Taylor again assembled the special train from the New York area and the guest list was just as long as the first trip to the banks of the Delaware River. As before, the guests — this time sporting red carnations and waving miniature Harvard University flags — were taken directly to the shipyard and assembled at the christening platform. For this ship the guest list was topped by Harvard President and Mrs. Charles Eliot. The role of naming the vessel was bestowed on their sixteen-year-old grand-daughter, Ruth Eliot, given honors equal to the *Yale*'s Miss Hadley (although there was no report of any jewelry). After the ship slipped smoothly into the waters of the Delaware, the visiting party again entrained for a gala luncheon on the trip back to New York.

June 29, 1907—

Although not all the fancy woodwork was finished, and some of the furnishings and equipment still were being installed, the *Yale* was ready for her first run over the Metropolitan Line's "outside route" to Boston.

On her maiden voyage with the still-new mode of propulsion, the *Yale* was to exhibit speeds never before seen on the heavily traveled route and set standards for future speedsters. Captain S.F. Pike was in command, while Andrew Fletcher himself was at the turbine controls.

Leaving the Hoboken, New Jersey, wharves of the Fletcher Company, *Yale* passed New York's South Ferry at 4:30 a.m. and was abreast of the Eastern Steamship Company's docks in Boston harbor at 6:18 p.m. for an official time of 13 hours, 47½ minutes. This included slow-downs while moving up the East River to Hell Gate, from Long Island Sound at Execution Rocks and the Race, over Nantucket Shoals and then around Cape Cod, with a reverse tide during part of the voyage. On the other hand, from Execution Light to Boston Light, a run of about twelve hours, Morse's new flyer averaged 21.45 knots (24.7 statute miles per hour) with a top speed of 24.32 knots (28 mph).

The *Yale*'s first voyage under her own power had taken place only two days earlier, on June 27, when her crew took her for builder's trials under the watchful eyes of Fletcher yard personnel, two runs down New York Bay to check out her workings. The *Nautical Gazette* reported all equipment functioned smoothly, and the high-speed propellers created no noticeable vibration in her hull. Noted the *Gazette*: "The large sideboard at the after end of the dining room, which is on the main deck aft, was filled with glassware, and there was not the slightest vibration or tinkle to be heard from same."

June 31, 1907 —

Since the *Harvard* would not be ready for service until later in the year, Morse decided to use *Yale* for a break-in period on his Eastern Steamship Company's international division between Boston and St. John, New Brunswick. Her first voyage took place only two days after her arrival from New York, with every stateroom booked.

The *Yale* would continue on the Canadian route until September, operating most of the time using only six boilers — her great speed was not a significant factor on the Boston-St. John run. She was able to maintain schedules with satisfactory passenger loads utilizing only half her power.

September 10, 1907 —

The *Harvard*'s first run to Boston was a little more dramatic than was the *Yale*'s. With Morse aboard and loaded with Metropolitan Line directors and guests, the second fast turbiner ran onto a rock while rounding Hallett's Point into Hell Gate. Perhaps it was prophetic that *Harvard*

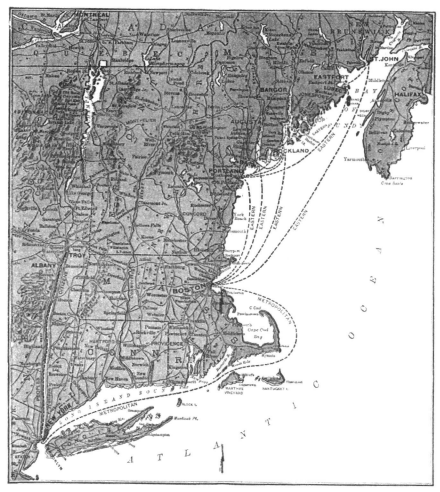

Until the launch of the Harvard *the* Yale *was put into service on Eastern's Boston-to-St. John service as shown on this brochure map. The Huntington Library*

would encounter rocks on her initial voyage — her last one would end on a rocky shore a continent away many years hence.

It also was ironic that Morse's nemesis would figure in the incident. A New Haven Railroad tugboat towing two barges in Hell Gate caused the *Harvard* to veer away toward the Astoria shore to avoid a collision, when she struck the rock. The *Harvard*'s crew was able to swing her off, but a strong flood tide swept her back on again — three times. Even so, there was no apparent damage to the steel hull and the ship continued on to Boston. However, the incident, plus a stretch of fog and reverse tides, meant the trip required 14 hours, 52 minutes. Still, the ship was ready to join her sister in alternating service on the New York-Boston run in only a week's time.

September 18, 1907 —
Metropolitan Line freighters had been operating on the route for fifty years, but Morse was now ready to launch his speedsters in head-to-head competition with Morgan's Fall River Line for the overnight passenger trade. The *Harvard* was poised at New York's Pier 45 and the *Yale* set to

Part of the Yale *and* Harvard's *speed is attributable to their sharp bows and narrow hulls as shown by this view of the* Yale *in drydock soon after her completion. Mariners' Museum, Newport News, Virginia, Elwin P. Eldredge Collection*

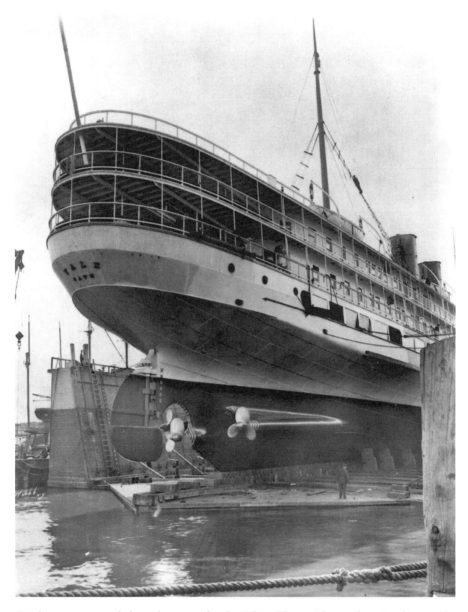

Triple screws provided ample power for the White Flyers. The worker standing on the drydock, lower right, provides an indication of the relative size of the vessel. The Mariners' Museum, Newport News, Virginia, Elwin M. Eldredge Collection

depart from the Eastern Steamship Line's India Wharf in Boston. Both ships cast off on the 337-mile voyage at the same hour, 5 p.m. The trip was scheduled for fifteen hours. The *Harvard*, with about 500 passengers, made the northbound voyage in fourteen hours flat, while the *Yale*, completely sold out, churned through the southbound segment in 13 hours, 53 minutes. The battle of the overnight boats was off to a flying start.

May 19, 1910—

The *Yale* and *Harvard* were designed as coal burners, but the growing use of oil as fuel for ship engines led the vessels' operators to make the switch, again placing the ships among the pioneers of maritime progress. Oil was more costly than coal, but there were other factors to consider. Coal burners were subject to New York's smoke ordinance, and the limited layover period made it difficult to load 235-240 tons of the rock-like black stuff, all to be hidden away in bunkers, not to mention how dirty coaling made the white liners.

Nonetheless, it would cost an extra $60,000 a year to burn oil instead, a high price for loading convenience. But also to be factored in was the reduced "black gang" in the fire rooms — not only a cost item, but also a continuing problem in obtaining a steady labor force for the physically debilitating, low-paying task.

To the *Yale* went the honor of being the first oil-burning passenger vessel to sail from the port of New York when her crew under Capt. Thomas Hawes cast off from Pier 9, North River, shortly before noon on May 19, 1910, for a demonstration run to the Ambrose Lightship. Instead of the forty-eight men required for the sweaty job of shoveling and trimming coal while stoking her fireboxes, only six men were controlling the pipes directing the flow of oil from her tanks to the ship's fires.

Reported the *New York Times*: "No attempt at speed was made, but she went along at about a land average of 17 knots with occasional bursts of 24 knots at an expenditure of 1,000 gallons of oil an hour." The paper quoted the consulting engineer, Robert MacGregor, as saying the engines were developing about 8,000 horsepower. Thirty-six burners had been installed, three under each of the ship's twelve boilers. Storage for 100,000 gallons of oil had been set up in the double bottoms.

"Down in the heat of the engine room the force of men was working apparently with little expenditure of energy," said the *Times* in describing the changing scene below deck. "They kept the oil supply running freely and the tanks filled, while the *Yale* met every demand made of her. All they had to do was to keep the oil burners under each of the big

ALL THE WAY BY WATER

By this service the Metropolitan Line has added another in what has become the most popular Summer route for passengers between New York and Boston.... The great popularity of this route for pleasure and commercial travel was insured from its inception in 1907. Thousands of its patrons have attested their appreciation of the service by traveling again and again upon the great Turbiners and the route has therefore become a fixed factor in the Transportation World....

The restaurants on the new Turbine Steamships *Yale* and *Harvard* ... compare favorably with those of your club or home ... the windows all look directly out to sea, thus enabling passengers to enjoy the picturesque scenery while they dine ... There is electric light and steam-heating equipment in the staterooms ...

Innovations on the *Yale* and *Harvard* are the smoking room and café on the hurricane deck and the dainty writing room in the Main Saloon. The Barber Shop is located on the main deck...while the book, periodical and newsstand is located in the Main Saloon forward.

In the *Yale* and *Harvard* there are more rooms equipped with private baths and toilet accessories than in any other steamships of their size in the country. The safety devices, sanitary plumbing, steam heating, ventilation and electrical equipment are the very latest and best obtainable, and in many respects the *Yale* and *Harvard* are unique and quite in advance of anything yet constructed.

— Metropolitan Line schedule, 1909

boilers going. It was a touch of the valve here and an increase of the supply of oil there to keep up the terrific heat so as to give a steady pressure on the turbines. The ease with which the oil is handled is one of the points in its favor."

Conversion of the *Harvard* followed on the heels of the demonstrated success of the changeover on the *Yale*.

August, 1910 —

Competition between the New Haven and the Metropolitan ships was intense, particularly in the summer months. Most revenues were earned from June to September. Rate cutting was standard practice. The New Haven cut its New York-Boston fare from $4 to $3.65 when the *Yale* and *Harvard* came on the scene, but restored it to $4 when they sailed away. (Steamer fares at the time included only the basic cost of passage. Staterooms, meals and other special services were extra. Free berths were available, but most passengers booked staterooms. An inside room cost $1, while the better-ventilated outside rooms went for $2 or $3.)

The turbiners' operating costs for a single trip during August, 1910, averaged a few cents over $1,995. Meanwhile, laying-up expenses at the end of the season were increasing, from $52,594 in 1908 to $65,923 in 1909.

September 21, 1910 —

Moves to eliminate the strong competitive assets that Charles W. Morse brought to the New England shipping scene culminated on September 21, 1910, when the Metropolitan Line announced that the *Yale* and *Harvard* not only would be withdrawn from service in October, but had been sold and would leave the east coast. It was said the vessels' new home port would be San Francisco. Only in later years would investigations reveal the role of the New Haven Railroad in the "exile" of the fast turbiners from the New York-Boston run to distant California ports.

Rumors of the sale of the two ships circulated almost from the day they steamed onto the shipping scene in 1907, especially since the collapse of Morse's Consolidated Steamship Lines, his $60 million umbrella operation, in the bank panic that year. By the following spring, J.P.

Postcards were a common form of advertising during the first part of the twentieth century. This one is unusual in that it is one of the few to show the Yale *under the Metropolitan Line house flag. Bill Stritzel collection.*

Morgan and his allies had achieved corporate positions in which they could influence affairs of the Metropolitan Steamship Company. Efforts to transfer the *Yale* and the *Harvard* to the west coast began almost immediately (Morgan could have purchased the ships, but was focused on clearing away competition from his rail-steamship combination involving the Fall River Line).

Reorganizations resulted in the formation of two Metropolitan Lines, one incorporated in New Jersey which owned the ships, and one in Maine which operated them. Negotiations for the coast-to-coast transfer stretched over 2½ years. Finally it was announced the ships would be leased to the Pacific Navigation Company (also a New Jersey corporation). Not until 1916 was it publicly disclosed that the true owner of the ships was the Metropolitan Line in which the New Haven's powerful influence had gained dominance. (In 1914, Morse's sister, Jennie R. Morse, charged in a lawsuit that the New Haven had arranged the lease of the turbiners to Pacific Navigation at a rate providing no profitable return to Metropolitan simply to get rid of the competition.)

PART II

WEST COAST SERVICE

5

CALIFORNIA
OR BUST

Overnight boats designed for rivers and lakes, or even for the New York-Boston run, were not expected to spend much time on the open sea. The *Harvard* and *Yale* did face the broad reaches of the North Atlantic for a short period during each run while rounding Cape Cod, but the operating season exposed them only during the most tranquil months of the year. (The *Yale*, of course, had operated for a brief time on the Boston-St. John run.) Now they had to be prepared for a perilous two-ocean voyage that would take them around South America, exposed to the full force of the weather gods.

With the *Yale*'s return to New York on October 2, 1910, the Boston service by the fast turbiners was terminated and work of preparing the ships for their voyage to the west coast began. Their lower decks, normally open, were boarded up to combat heavy seas. Only a few months after being converted to oil burners, each vessel underwent a partial reconversion to coal. Six firerooms reverted to coal because of the greater availability of that fuel at South American ports.

With fuel conversion and hull preparations completed as quickly as possible, *Yale* and *Harvard* sat anchored off Staten Island while a crew was arranged for the long trip and supplies were brought aboard. Each

Color postcards were a popular advertising medium at the time. The two ships were so similar in appearance that the title on the card at right claims the ship is the Harvard *yet clearly it is the* Yale. *Steamship Historical Society of America (Albert E. Gayer collection).*

The Yale *approaches the dock on one of her last runs on the east coast. Steamship Historical Society of America, George W. Hilton Collection*

In this stern view of the Yale *it is clear how vulnerable the lower decks could be to heavy seas during the voyage around South America to Los Angeles. They were boarded up to prevent damage. Steamship Historical Society of America (Grayham Collection).*

ship was manned by eighty-four men, with the *Harvard* commanded by Capt. John J. Shea, a San Francisco bar pilot sent east for the express purpose of bringing her west. The first officer was Henry M. Speyer, scheduled to become an official of the new line in San Francisco. The *Yale*'s skipper was Capt. A.E. Gove and his first officer was Capt. T.D. McFarland, slated to take over the *Yale* when Gove returned to the east coast.

"The two vessels looked different from the trim craft they were while on the Boston run," declared the *New York Times*. "Along each side are rows of heavy timber ... to prevent the seas from making inboard. More heavy timber is included to shore up the sides against the sea and everything moveable on the decks has been lashed down."

The newspaper reported all members of the crew looked forward to having a "good time" on the voyage. This was assured, said the *Times*, because the equipment aboard each ship included "two decks of cards, some checkers and chessboards."

Men of the *Harvard* had one passenger they felt was a good omen. "Varsity," the ship's pumpkin-colored cat, had long been a regular on the ship, but it was decided to put her ashore before the long voyage began. After being rowed to a dock three days before sailing time, the cat was discovered back aboard, curled up in a comfortable spot in the saloon.

No one solved the mystery of how "Varsity" negotiated her way back aboard the ship riding at anchor in the stream, but she was allowed to stay. "We believe the cat's return means good luck," said a crew member.

It is paradoxical that the western exile of the two ships engineered by a powerhouse railroad would put them into another competitive situation in which rail interests played key roles. As in the east, railroads used maritime subsidiaries to gain footholds on the west coast, where the Southern Pacific controlled most of the rails.

The geography of the continent's western shoreline limited the major American ports to Seattle/Tacoma in Washington, Portland in Oregon, and San Francisco, Los Angeles/San Pedro and San Diego in California. The dominant line in both passengers and freight was the Pacific Coast Steamship Company, whose antecedents dated to 1860. Another, the Pacific Mail Steamship Company, furnished monthly service between Astoria, Oregon, at the mouth of the Columbia River, and the Isthmus of Panama (delivering mail under government contract, hence the name).

Later arrivals on the scene were the San Francisco and Portland Steamship Company (known as the "Big 3" for the number of vessels it operated between those ports) and the Great Northern Pacific Steamship Company. The Big 3 was the Union Pacific's subsidiary transporting passengers and freight into San Francisco — by 1915 it carried 55,000 persons

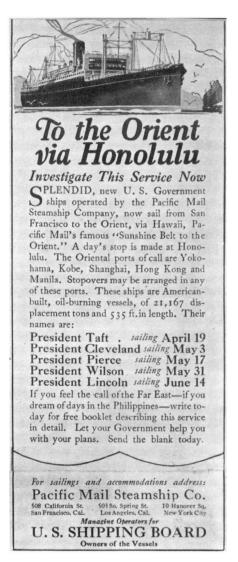

To the Orient via Honolulu

Investigate This Service Now

SPLENDID, new U. S. Government ships operated by the Pacific Mail Steamship Company, now sail from San Francisco to the Orient, via Hawaii, Pacific Mail's famous "Sunshine Belt to the Orient." A day's stop is made at Honolulu. The Oriental ports of call are Yokohama, Kobe, Shanghai, Hong Kong and Manila. Stopovers may be arranged in any of these ports. These ships are American-built, oil-burning vessels, of 21,167 displacement tons and 535 ft. in length. Their names are:

President Taft . *sailing* April 19
President Cleveland *sailing* May 3
President Pierce *sailing* May 17
President Wilson *sailing* May 31
President Lincoln *sailing* June 14

If you feel the call of the Far East—if you dream of days in the Philippines—write today for free booklet describing this service in detail. Let your Government help you with your plans. Send the blank today.

For sailings and accommodations address:

Pacific Mail Steamship Co.

508 California St. 503 So. Spring St. 10 Hanover Sq.
San Francisco, Cal. Los Angeles, Cal. New York City

Managing Operators for

U. S. SHIPPING BOARD

Owners of the Vessels

Pacific Mail Steamship Company, which also ran to the Far East, was but one of many lines with which the White Flyers would compete. Author's collection

As in the east, railroads controlled most transportation routes in the west, including the water routes. The Great Northern Railroad ran the Great Northern Pacific Steamship Company. The Pacific Coast Steamship Company, listed in newspaper ad at left, was the dominant player in the coastwise market.   Author's collection

a year. The Great Northern Pacific was an operation of the Great Northern and Northern Pacific Railroads, utilizing two ships from Portland to Los Angeles.

The Pacific Steamship Company, also known as the Admiral Line, was the pride of Hubbard Foster Alexander. It, too, would compete with, and eventually take over both the Yale *and* Harvard*'s west coast operations. Author's collection*

Like Charles W. Morse's short period of ascendency in eastern shipping, the west had its counterpart in the person of Hubbard Foster Alexander. But H.F. Alexander, as he preferred to be called, was to play a much more influential and enduring role in Pacific maritime affairs and was to be closely involved in the western chapters of the four-decade saga of the *Harvard* and *Yale*.

Born in Colorado in 1879, Alexander started at fourteen as a dockworker in Tacoma and rose to become president of several steamship lines, combining his operations under the label of the Admiral Line (his house flag was a Maltese cross surrounded by a grouping of white stars on a field of blue, and the line's motto was "Safety, Courtesy and Food.")

When the Pacific Navigation Company's plans to send the *Harvard* and *Yale* west were made public, Alexander was ready to enhance his competitive situation by forging an arrangement with Pacific Navigation to route passengers and freight over each other's lines with through tickets and bills of lading, and with arrivals and departures arranged so passengers would not have to stay overnight in San Francisco. The White Flyers would traverse the San Francisco-Los Angeles leg in less than nineteen hours, while the competition took twenty-three to twenty-five hours. By 1914, the twin liners would be carrying 120,000 passengers annually, but would seek the Interstate Commerce Commission's help in forcing the Southern Pacific, the Santa Fe, the Western Pacific and the Salt Lake Railroads to make the same arrangement with Pacific Navigation in establishing through routes and joint fares as they had with the Pacific Coast Steamship Company and the Big 3.

But those battles were still in the future. With each vessel buttoned up for the long voyage, the *Yale* and *Harvard* took their departure from New York harbor and the northeast competitive wars on October 17, 1910. Ahead lay a two-month voyage to unknown waters. A new life awaited the fast turbiners on an unfamiliar coast a continent away.

This rare photo shows the White Flyers just after their arrival on the West Coast in 1910. An undeveloped Terminal Island is in the background. Leon Calloway Collection

6

PACIFIC DATEBOOK
I

December 16, 1910 —

Plans to quickly embark the fast turbiners on their new San Francisco-Los Angeles service were in place even before they arrived at San Pedro to a tumultuous welcome led by the local chamber of commerce (still functioning even though the port was now a part of a consolidated metropolis of greater Los Angeles).

The *Harvard* and the *Yale* tied up at the East San Pedro wharf on Terminal Island on December 16, 1910, after an uneventful 14,000-mile voyage from New York that included calls at the island of St. Lucia; Rio de Janeiro, Brazil; Montevideo, Uruguay and Punta Arenas, Chile, before the ships transited the Strait of Magellan and stopped at Coronel and Tocopilla in Chile and Lobitos, Peru, in the Pacific. The ships were reported to have stayed within sight of each other for the entire trip. (*Harvard* set a communications record by sending a wireless message to Coney Island, New York, while the two ships were off Manzanillo, Mexico, 3,000 miles to the southwest.)

Before the ships even arrived on the western shore, the Salt Lake Railroad — seeking to enhance its competitive strength against the

The Pacific Navigation Company operated the ships out of San Pedro. The Salt Lake Railroad ran trains from downtown scheduled to meet the White Flyers as they loaded and discharged their passengers. The Huntington Library

Southern Pacific — had arranged for special trains of parlor cars and day coaches to run from downtown Los Angeles to dockside in about an hour's time. The Pacific Navigation Company, the new operator, was anxious to get the service under way, but first the ships had to be stripped of their extra shielding and spruced up for the first regular voyage north.

Work was rushed in cleaning the ships, and while stores and provisions were taken aboard the stewards department was setting in place wholesale quantities of dishes, glassware and linens. The tasks were completed in less than four days and the *Yale* sailed on her inaugural west coast trip on December 20. The operators quickly learned they needed to do a better job of advertising subsequent sailings — fewer than 200 passengers were aboard for the trip. (The San Pedro Chamber of Commerce

The Harvard *and the* Yale *soon became popular with coastwise travelers. Here the* Harvard *shows more black smoke than economic operation would dictate, but she is making good speed, the key to the ships' success. San Francisco Maritime National Historical Park, Walter A. Scott Collection*

would help; it was readying a ship model patterned after the *Yale* and the *Harvard* for the year-end Tournament of Roses parade in nearby Pasadena to spread word of the vessels' arrival.)

December 21, 1910 —

The sleek white liner *Yale* brought the "overnight boat" concept to California travel when San Francisco bar pilot Capt. John J. Shea steamed

The Harvard *outbound in 1912 from San Pedro past the Angels Gate lighthouse on its eighteen hour run to San Francisco. Leon Callaway Collection*

her through the Golden Gate to her Pacific Street pier at 10:30 a.m. after an eighteen-hour voyage. (Shea transferred from the *Harvard* for the first trip north.) The *San Francisco Chronicle* noted the event, declaring shipping interests predicted the two vessels "will almost revolutionize the coastwise passenger traffic."

Speed over the water was a key to success, but so was a quick turn-around. The *Yale* exhibited this when she departed on the first south-bound leg at 5 p.m. on the 21st, just six and-a-half hours after her arrival that morning. The passenger load had improved — there were 450 travelers aboard. The list included the new line's first honeymoon couple, Mr. and Mrs. H.L. Smith, sent on their voyage by a party of friends "with showers of rice and words of good luck."

December 24, 1910 —

With the *Yale*'s return to San Pedro, it now was the *Harvard*'s turn to make her inaugural run, with veteran Pacific Coast Capt. Rasmus Jepson in command. Christmas Eve was not the best starting date, but eighty passengers must have felt it appropriate to arrive in San Francisco the next morning in plenty of time for Christmas dinner. One hundred passengers were aboard when *Harvard* slipped away from the Pacific Street wharf at 4:20 p.m. that afternoon bound for Los Angeles (perhaps somewhat apologetically — the ship had jammed her bow into the Jackson Street dock, causing some damage to the piling and timbers).

The Harvard *on San Francisco Bay passes an outward bound three-masted sailing ship, a rare photo graphically showing steam replacing sail. San Francisco Maritime National Historical Park (Morton-Waters collection)*

The Harvard *departing San Diego for the trip north, circa 1911. Note the period naval vessel in the background. San Diego Historical Society Photograph Collection*

March 3, 1911 —

The White Flyers quickly settled into a routine, each making four round trips a week. The new year was little more than two months old before each vessel was adding a swing south to San Diego to the week's schedule. The ships set a high standard for comfort and ease in coastal travel, almost matching the trip time by train. A northbound trip went like this: passengers would sail from San Diego at 9 a.m., reaching San Pedro at 2 p.m. By 3 p.m. the *Yale* or the *Harvard* was due to depart for San Francisco, reaching that city by 9:30 a.m. the following morning. The southbound voyage would depart at 4 p.m. When scheduled for San Diego, the ships would arrive in San Pedro at 10 a.m., depart for the southern city at 3 o'clock and reach San Diego at 8 p.m.

The San Diego leg cost only $2. The Los Angeles-San Francisco fare was $8.35, while a berth cost 50 cents or $1, depending on location. Rooms were $1, $3 and $4, depending on facilities which in some instances included brass beds, while the deluxe cabins with private bath went for $6 and $8. As had been the practice on the New York-Boston run, meals were a la carte, but a dinner could be purchased for about a dollar. Pacific Navigation's prices were slightly higher than other shipping lines, but the speed of the White Flyers and the ambiance was considered worth the difference.

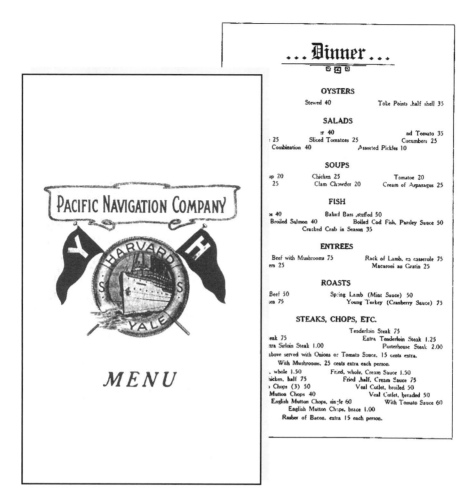

The White Flyers' menus offered variety, quality and decent prices for the time. A la carte meals were standard. The Huntington Library

John M. Houston, in his history, *It Happened in San Pedro*, notes the hold the two ships took on Californians, particularly those in southern cities:

> One of the most exciting pleasures of an earlier day…was a voyage on either the S.S. *Harvard* or *Yale* … No steamer has been seen on the west coast since their day that has claimed such affection, and when both ships were tied up at their East San Pedro wharf (Terminal Island) all eyes were drawn to their long white, clean lines. It was everyone's ambition to sail on one of the collegiate twins someday.

The Yale, *left, and* Harvard *tied to their wharf at San Pedro's Terminal Island never failed to draw the attention of passersby during their early west coast years. The four-masted schooner* John A. Campbell *right offers another comparison of the old with the new. San Francisco Maritime National Historical Park, Photographic Collection*

Houston describes a typical departure in the years before World War I: "As the *Yale* cast off with a warning blast from its deep-throated whistle which echoed from San Pedro Hill, the little orchestra in the lounge played as loudly as it could, for most of the passengers were now on deck to wave at their friends as if it were a trip to Hawaii or Hong Kong." (The gala departures at each port were to become standard features of the ships' operations. The happy scene, replete with music, deep blasts from the ship's whistle, colorful confetti, and windblown waves of serpentine, would live on in the memories of those who witnessed such events.)

Dancing to the ship's orchestra was a nightly feature, and the colorful public rooms were places where many travelers made new

Whenever one of the ships departed, bands played, friends of passengers gathered on the pier and confetti and serpentine flew as if the voyage would last several weeks rather than overnight. Here the Yale *moves down San Diego Bay after just such a departure. San Diego Historical Society, Photograph Collection*

acquaintances overnight. The brightly lit ships — operating almost as "commute" vessels up and down the California coastal route — often were clearly visible from the darkened shore along the sparsely populated sections of land between the state's two major cities. Sleep was almost the last thing a traveler thought about, unless the trip really was strictly business.

January 24, 1912 —

The schedules under which the two ships operated were so finely tuned that the slightest problem could throw them out of sync. On this date the *Harvard* did not arrive in San Francisco in the morning, but after dark that night. A line which became entangled around one of the ship's three propellers had to be removed by the crew while the ship lay to off the Southern California coast. A quick turnaround at the San Francisco pier sent the *Harvard* back into the night at top speed to repair the broken schedule.

July 31, 1916 —

The year 1916 was a highly successful one for H.F. Alexander. Not only had operations of his Admiral Line continued to grow, but his rail-magnate competitors suffered serious losses through shipwreck and fire, further strengthening his competitive position. On July 31 Alexander consolidated his California presence by announcing his Pacific-Alaska Navigation Company would lease the *Harvard* and the *Yale* from their

This view of the Harvard *at San Pedro gives one a sense of the other types of harbor traffic found on a typical day in the era before World War I. San Francisco Maritime National Historical Park, Randolph Brandt Photographic Collection*

The Harvard *throws out her usual cloud of black smoke as she approaches a pier in San Francisco on the northern terminus of her route. San Francisco Maritime National Historical Park, Morton-Waters Photographic Collection.*

The Harvard *on San Francisco Bay during the time she was chartered to Admiral Line as shown by the insignia on her stacks. San Francisco Maritime National Historical Park* S.F. Call-Bulletin *Photographic Collection*

true owners, revealed for the first time to be the Metropolitan Line of New Jersey. Their subsidiary, the Pacific Navigation Company, would be dissolved.

Admiral Line's charter would run for five years, to September, 1921, with an option to renew for an additional five years. Alexander would pay Metropolitan a minimum of $30,000 a month as long as both ships were running, with a formula specifying how expenses would be divided.

The year 1916 was a good one for the fast turbiners as well. The Great War in Europe had created a global shipping shortage, which reduced the number of passenger vessels traversing the Pacific Coast. The *Yale* and *Harvard* passenger lists were long that summer. On one run to San Diego, *Harvard* carried 802 travelers.

September 1, 1916 —

A new era in the lives of the *Harvard* and the *Yale* began with their link to shipping magnate H.F. Alexander and his Admiral Line. Little changed aboard the ships or their operations. They were still the "flying sisters," distinguished by their white hulls. But as of September 1, 1916, their raked smokestacks, previously all black, henceforth bore the buff color that set off the Alexander ships. And they flew the Admiral Line's blue banner with its Maltese Cross and field of white stars.

There were practical changes as well. The San Francisco terminal moved from Pier 7 to Pier 24, where Alexander's offices were located. More important, fares now included all meals, as was the standard practice on most steamship lines. One-way tickets, now including meals and a berth, were still $8.35 to Los Angeles and $10.15 to San Diego, with round trips for $14 and $17. Display ads in the *San Francisco Chronicle* proclaimed "perfect service" to Los Angeles every Monday, Wednesday, Friday and Saturday, and to San Diego every Monday, Wednesday and Friday.

It appeared the *Harvard* and the *Yale* were set for a long association with the Pacific shipping powerhouse. But a bigger operator came on the scene with plans for the ships that their owners and designers never dreamed of.

PART III

WORLD WAR I

7

OVER THERE —
AND HALFWAY BACK

By the time the United States entered World War I on April 6, 1917, as a result of Germany's resumption of unrestricted submarine warfare, the world shipping situation was so tight that American vessels were in short supply, hull valuations were sky high and ship operators prospered while attempting to fill global demand for passenger and freight sailings. Now the U.S. Navy added its requirements to the ship shortage.

Still, almost a year passed before the Navy turned its sights on the fast turbiners. Perhaps it was not until American troops were a reality in the trenches of France that the need for fast, short-run transports in the English Channel became a priority in Washington. Although some thought was given to converting the *Yale* and *Harvard* into superfast minelayers, it was decided they best could serve as short-haul troopships. That was to be their role, creating the "Channel Express" that would be remembered proudly for the remainder of their active lives.

Early in March, 1918, the Navy Department commandeered the two vessels, later taking full ownership by purchasing them for $1,420,000. The commandant of the 12th Naval District at San Francisco took possession of the *Yale* and delivered her to the Mare Island Navy Yard on March 13 for conversion. The *Harvard*, then undergoing turbine overhaul at the

65

The Harvard *completes her makeover as USS* Charles *at Mare Island Navy Yard on June 1, 1918. The main changes were the construction of a flying bridge on top of the wheelhouse, the addition of crow's nests on the masts and, of course, the "dazzle" paint scheme designed to confuse observers. U.S. Naval Historical Center*

Union Iron Works shipyard in San Francisco Bay, was taken over on March 21 and ultimately towed to Mare Island for a similar makeover. The *Yale* (assigned the hull number SD-1672) was commissioned on March 25 under her existing name, but the *Harvard* would get a new one (the Navy already had a *Harvard*, the steel yacht *Wacouta*, renamed and commissioned on May 10, 1917). The fast turbiner was commissioned on April 9 as the USS *Harvard* (SP-1298), but two days later the name was changed to the USS *Charles*, the same as the broad river that borders Harvard University.

Work on converting the coastal liners into workhorse troopers began immediately, first on USS *Yale*, then on USS *Charles*. The ships were stripped of their civilian amenities and interior spaces adapted to house a permanent crew, as well as passengers in bulk. (Some of the quality wooden furniture was taken ashore to Mare Island's shops and offices, where it was reported to still be in evidence decades later.)

Crews were assigned almost immediately, but housed ashore until yard workers could construct suitable living spaces aboard. Two naval reserve officers, Lt. Cmdrs. Richard C. Brennan and M.F. Tarpey, were designated as captains of USS *Yale* and USS *Charles*, respectively. (They were to remain in command throughout the ships' overseas service.) The complement of each ship consisted of twelve wardroom officers, eight chief petty officers and 193 men. The crews, made up at the Naval Training Camp at Mare Island, were mustered aboard on April 23.

Yard workers converted 118 cabins for officer passengers, but the bulk of the space was arranged to provide seating accommodations for short runs across the English Channel. Once again the ships' fuel systems were refitted to permit the use of coal, available in ample supply in Britain. Six boilers were converted and bunker space for 600 tons of coal was provided. With the ships' maximum oil capacity of 2,500 barrels, each vessel then had an operational range of about 2,500 miles.

Exteriors were changed with the addition of a flying bridge on the roof of the original pilot house which extended the full width of each ship. Small crows' nests also were added to each of the two masts. But the most obvious change in the fast turbiners' civilian décor was the new paint job. The hulls, famous for their distinctive spotless white appearance, were painted in the Navy's multi-colored zig-zag "dazzle" camouflage scheme then in favor. The instant recognition of the White Flyers was gone for the duration.

USS *Yale* left San Francisco Bay on May 18, 1918, en route to the Atlantic Coast, but with a naval chore to be performed en route. In addition to a draft of sailors picked up during a stop for oil in San Diego, she carried fifteen marines to be delivered to the American Legation in Managua, Nicaragua. After an earlier stop in Acapulco, *Yale* delivered the marines and official mail to the consulate at Corinto, Nicaragua, and then proceeded to Panama.

The *Yale*'s return to Atlantic waters was far simpler than her westward voyage around South America nearly eight years earlier. The Panama Canal now was in service and the trooper made short work of the transit after first refilling her bunkers from a coal barge at Balboa. As she moved north in the Atlantic warnings came of German submarine activity and *Yale* assumed full war status. (The German sub *U-151* was active along the eastern seaboard and had sunk six schooners and three steamships in the previous week.) Fortunately, *Yale* reached Hampton Roads, Virginia,

U-151 *as she appeared in 1917. She was a threat to USS* Yale. *After the war she was given to the French as part of their reparations and later sunk as a target.* Conway's All the World's Fighting Ships, *Aldo Fraccaroli Collection*

USS Charles *loads troops for France at Southampton, England on September 27, 1918. Troops can be seen boarding at the midships gangway. Detail of the flying bridge added at Mare Island can clearly be seen in this photo. U.S. Naval Historical Center*

without incident late on June 3 and entered the Portsmouth Navy Yard on June 5 to complete conversion and repairs.

Meanwhile, USS *Charles*, after undergoing changes at Mare Island matching those made on *Yale*, departed San Francisco Bay on June 1 and caught up with her sister ship at Hampton Roads on June 26. Both embarked troops and sailed on July 10 in a convoy bound for Brest, France, reaching that port for the first time on July 23 (they were herded en route by a familiar vessel — the convoy flagship was the west coast liner USS *Matsonia*). After quick trips to Plymouth and Portsmouth, England, the fast turbiners were directed to "operate under orders of the British Principal Transport Officer, Southampton." The Channel Express was ready to get underway.

Now USS *Yale* and USS *Charles* began shuttle services reminiscent of their New York-Boston and San Francisco-Los Angeles runs. Operating separately mostly from Southampton beginning July 26, the sisters sailed almost daily to Le Havre, Boulogne or Brest in France, voyages of less than ten hours, with about five more for turnaround time. Sometimes they carried as many as 2,500 passengers to the continent, sometimes the westbound total was zero. Most often a British destroyer or "P" boat provided an escort, but occasionally the ships traveled alone.

SS YALE CREW SENDS GREETING TO S.F. FOLK ...

The *Chronicle* has received the following letter, with the request that it be published, from the crew of the steamer Yale, formerly engaged in coastwise passenger service between San Francisco and Los Angeles and now in the service of the United States Navy in European waters. Dotted lines indicate passages slashed out by the censor:

U.S. Naval Forces, Operating in European Waters,
Nov. 25, 1918

To the People of San Francisco — Dear Friends:

Just a few lines from a ship which all of you, no doubt, remember well, though you may have forgotten it in the rush of war. It is the SS Yale, formerly a passenger carrier between San Francisco and Los Angeles, and now one of, if not the busiest ... in Uncle Sam's service, for we have a record of ... trips, which we believe is second to none. We sailed from San Francisco May 16, 1918, and since that time have been busy practically day and night ... who are beating the Huns. We have carried in the neighborhood ... which we think is a record we may well be proud of. Also, we have never laid up a day for repairs. So when you think of the men who are fighting to make the world safe for democracy, don't forget the boys in blue who have made it possible for them to fight, for we had the job ... most treacherous and dangerous stretch of water to be found and though we call our kitchen the galley and wear our trousers upside down, we have been true to our trust.

We are proud to say that we are a California ship and a California crew, comprised chiefly of boys from San Francisco and vicinity, and when it is all over over here we are coming back to the city of the Golden Gate which we all love so well. So dear friends, kindly keep a spot in your hearts warm for us. To the people of San Francisco who have lost friends and relatives on account of the epidemic of influenza, we extend our most heartfelt sympathy, for we know what it means to lose those who we hold dear.

Hoping this will reach you soon, we will close wishing you a Merry Christmas and a Happy New Year, and hoping that we may all be there to spend the next one with you.

Sincerely yours,
THE BOYS OF THE USS YALE

—San Francisco Chronicle, 12/22/18

The contribution of Pacific Steamship Co. to the war effort is shown in this World War I postcard. Their two ships, Harvard *and* Yale *bracket a field of stars indicating the 153 men who served in the armed forces. Bill Stritzel Collection*

The war ended on November 11, 1918, but not the workhorse roles for the White Flyers. Their shuttle runs continued well into the following year. For USS *Yale*, the total was eighty-five round trips, thirty-one during the final weeks of the war and fifty-four after the Armistice until April 29, 1919. How the flow was reversed is shown by these statistics: Until the Armistice, from Southampton to France, 72,145 persons, including 3,679 Army and Navy officers; after the Armistice, 27,201 persons, including 2,078 officers; total for all eastbound trips, 99,346. For westbound voyages to Southampton, the total before the Armistice was 7,936, including 729 officers; after the Armistice it was 104,111, including 3,363 officers. The westbound figure of 112,047 brought USS *Yale*'s total passenger load to 211,393. The bulk were American and British soldiers, but also included American and British Navy men, British WAACs, YMCA and Red Cross representatives, French Army and Navy men, French civilians, and a smattering of troops from the Italian, Portuguese, Belgian, Serbian and Polish Armies. Even German and Austrian prisoners of war were transported — 3,516 of them.

The USS *Charles*' record paralleled that of her sister ship. From her first cross-channel run on August 2, 1918, until the last on May 5, 1919, she made about sixty round trips and transported a total of 157,384 persons, with the passenger lists matching USS *Yale*'s in variety.

With military traffic much reduced, the Channel Express was disbanded and the sister ships were ordered home, but on separate routes.

The USS *Yale* left Southampton on May 1, 1919, touched at Plymouth to pick up freight for the USS *Hannibal*, and delivered it at Brest on May 3. Then, loaded with forty-one U.S. Army officers, 250 enlisted men, four YMCA secretaries, two Red Cross workers and one civilian, she departed on May 6 for New York.

The crossing was not to be an easy one — on May 9 USS *Yale* encountered a heavy sea. Water cascading over her forecastle carried away her starboard rail and smashed in the starboard side of her forward deckhouse. The ship slowed while a repair party made necessary patches, then she proceeded to Ponta Delgada in the Azores, arriving late on May 12. When she departed early on May 16, USS *Yale* not only was shipshape again, but had picked up eight more passengers. The remainder of the trip was uneventful, the ship reaching anchorage at Wehawken, New Jersey, on May 22, 1919.

The route of the USS *Charles* was somewhat different. She left Southampton on May 5, 1919, and swung up the English Channel to Antwerp and Rotterdam. After picking up 172 merchant marine passengers (from crews of Dutch ships taken over and operated by the United States Shipping Board during the war), she sailed from Rotterdam on May 26 and touched at Plymouth and Brest, where she took aboard 187 officers and men for transport home. USS *Charles* also stopped at the Azores and reached New York on June 18.

8

ATLANTIC
DATEBOOK
II

Although back in home waters, USS *Yale* and USS *Charles* still were thought to be of value to the Navy. For the time being they were needed for short passenger runs, and experts had to decide whether there was a role for the ships in the peacetime fleet.

One of the specialty vessels then in the planning stages was the aircraft carrier. While deciding the future of the fast turbiners, some thought was given to converting USS *Yale* and USS *Charles* into what was described as "heavier than air aviation tenders." Like the scheme to make them into fast minelayers, the idea never came to fruition. Instead, the Navy converted the 11,500-ton, twin-screw collier *Jupiter*, adding a wood-plank flight deck and commissioning her as the USS *Langley* (CV-1) on April 21, 1920. (The *Langley*, powered by turbines and electric drive, had a top speed of fifteen knots. It would have been interesting to see how much *Yale* and *Charles*, steaming into the wind at better than twenty knots, would have helped the lumbering biplanes of the day crawl their way aloft.)

May 27, 1919 —

The Navy had sailing orders for USS *Yale*, but first she needed an

An early biplane takes off from USS Langley *(CV-1) at San Diego in 1926. But for the luck of the draw, this might have been the fate of USS* Yale *and USS* Charles, *which were considered for conversion. U.S. Naval Photographic Center*

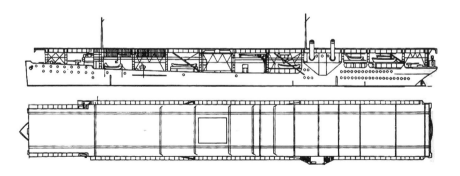

As completed USS Langley *carried twelve fighters, twelve spotters, six torpedo bombers and six seaplanes. Her turbo-electric drive was rated at 6,500 horsepower and produced 15.5 knots with two propellers.* Conway's All the World's Fighting Ships, 1906-1921

overhaul of her accommodations after the wear and tear of the Channel runs. She was moved to Pier 16, Hoboken, where thirty carpenters and eleven laborers swarmed aboard and started general repairs. Replacements for most of the crew came aboard. USS *Charles*, meanwhile, was moved to the Philadelphia Navy Yard, where she remained in ordinary until decommissioned on June 10, 1920.

June 1, 1919 —

USS *Yale* is attached to the Cruiser and Transport Force, North Atlantic Fleet. On June 7 her captain, newly promoted Cmdr. Richard C. Brennan, was succeeded by Lt. Cmdr. Frank C. Lane. The remainder of a new crew came aboard and *Yale* was ready to resume trooper duty, transporting mostly Army personnel.

June 10, 1919 —

USS *Yale*'s domestic transport service got off to an ignominious start. Embarkation of Army troops began at 8 a.m. and two hours later the soldiers were ordered off and the ship placed in quarantine — some of the passengers had been exposed to smallpox. The ship was quickly unloaded, including all supplies and baggage. All spaces were disinfected, the crew vaccinated and an armed guard placed about the ship. Remaining in quarantine for five days, USS *Yale* finally departed from Hoboken on her first domestic run, to Portsmouth, Virginia, with 1,515 passengers.

For the next month USS *Yale* moved swiftly up and down the mid-Atlantic coast, transporting service personnel between New York and Hoboken, and Hampton Roads, Newport News and Norfolk in Virginia. During the period she carried 9,482 passengers, including 230 officers. (One load was 700 naval prisoners, loaded from lighters off Deer Island. USS *Yale* delivered them to Cape May, New Jersey, where trawlers transshipped them to Cold Spring Inlet for discharge.)

July 19, 1919 —

At this point, the onetime White Flyers were under serious consideration for conversion to carriers. USS *Yale* received orders to proceed to the Philadelphia Navy Yard and report to the Commandant of the Fourth Naval District for inspection by a joint board and transfer from the Army to the Navy account. Her orders read "to be placed in ordinary pending and during conversion into a heavier-than-air craft carrier."

Here USS St. Louis *(Cruiser No. 20) is shown before World War I in gray paint adopted at the end of 1908. She was built as a "semi-armored cruiser" with a light waterline armor belt. U.S. Naval Photographic Center*

July 21, 1919 —

The *Yale* reached Philadelphia Navy Yard, underwent an examination by a Board of Inspection to complete the takeover from Army troopship jurisdiction, and went alongside the USS *St. Louis*. In doing so, USS *Yale*'s bow struck the cruiser's starboard side a few feet forward of her armor plating, scratching the paint and snapping off a wooden beam. USS *Yale*'s jackstaff was carried away. It was an embarrassing end to her last seagoing voyage as a ship of the fleet.

September 3, 1919 —

Towed by two tugs, USS *Yale* was moved to the Navy Yard's Back Channel and moored alongside her sister ship, USS *Charles*. They were to remain there for the rest of their World War I-era service careers. The ships were listed as "in ordinary" and crews were materially reduced.

November 11, 1919 —

The first anniversary of the Armistice was observed aboard the fast turbiners with receipt of the news that instead of a future in the Navy's new air service, the vessels were being ordered sold.

April 21, 1920 —

West Coast shipping tycoon H.F. Alexander had barely started operating the *Yale* and the *Harvard* under the colors of his Admiral Line when the Navy took them away. Even though the purchase had been outright, there was the standard practice of repurchasing ships (at a reduced price) in peacetime. Everyone assumed Alexander's Pacific Steamship Company (the Admiral Line) would be in the forefront of any bidding war — and would win. It turned out to be a wrong assumption.

The Navy tried selling the sister ships three times, rejecting bids in the first two sales because they were too low. The successful bidder, on April 21, 1920, was the Edward P. Farley Company of Chicago, representing a group of Southern California businessmen and civic leaders known as the "Yale-Harvard Syndicate." Their avowed purpose was to "promote maritime commerce out of Los Angeles harbor." Pacific Steamship was among the bidders, as were other interests. But the Los Angeles group was tops with a bid of $1,755,000 — just $55,000 more than the appraised value the Navy required.

June 10, 1920 —

Both ships were placed out of commission.

June 17, 1920 —

The *Yale* and the *Charles*, returned to "civilian" status, departed from Philadelphia en route to the Pacific Coast via the Panama Canal. Their Atlantic-to-Pacific route would be much shorter and easier the second time.

PART IV

RETURN TO THE PACIFIC

9

PACIFIC

DATEBOOK

II

July 10, 1920 —

After stops in Jacksonville, Florida; Colon, Panama, and Salina Cruz, Mexico, the *Charles* reached California first, arriving in San Pedro's outer harbor at dawn July 10, 1920, and finally docking about noon to a welcoming medley of ships' whistles and cheers of civic greeters. Two days later it was the turn of the *Yale*, 600 miles behind because of a fuel shortage in the Canal Zone. The *Charles* did not waste any time resuming her former identity, switching her name back to *Harvard* on July 29. But much had changed in the time the White Flyers had been away at war. The ships' new owners had not yet formally organized, new port arrangements had to be developed — and the ships themselves required major reconstruction before they could meet their own pre-war standards (the new owners indicated they planned to spend $1,500,000 restoring the two vessels). Months would pass before they were ready.

The first order of business was formal establishment of the company leadership. The Yale-Harvard Syndicate filed papers of incorporation on June 8, 1920, as the Los Angeles Steamship Company, known ever since as the LASSCO Line, with the objective of first providing service to San

Francisco and later extending its business to Hawaii and the Far East. On August 23 operations were combined with the Los Angeles Pacific Navigation Company, which had similar transpacific aspirations.

The principal stockholders of LASSCO were Fred L. Baker, Gen. M.H. Sherman, Erle M. Leaf, Mericos H. Whittier, Frank R. Seaver and Harry and Ralph Chandler. A.J. Frey, long active in Pacific Coast shipping, was appointed general manager. The Chandlers were part of the leadership of the *Los Angeles Times*, Harry as president and general manager. His nephew, Ralph Chandler, had operated ships out of San Diego and a shipyard in Los Angeles; he later succeeded Frey as LASSCO general manager. Sherman was involved in forming the Los Angeles Railway, the first electric streetcars in the area. Whittier, an oil man, was the developer of Beverly Hills. Leaf and Seaver were attorneys. Baker, president of the Baker Iron Works, had helped organize the Los Angeles Chamber of Commerce and the Automobile Club of Southern California. These men also were active in the formation of the Los Angeles Shipbuilding and Drydock Company, Southern California's first, in 1917. Now that yard, and Chandler's, would undertake the project of rebuilding the *Yale* and the *Harvard* for their postwar careers.

During the next several months the fast turbiners underwent major hull changes that materially reduced a negative factor from the past — vibration. As built, each ship's lone steel deck extended back only as far as the forward boiler room bulkhead, the remainder being constructed of wood. This portion was removed and replaced with a steel deck after the steel frames supporting it were reinforced and stiffened. About 275 tons of steel was added to the ships, greatly strengthening the hulls and reducing the vibration from the turbines and triple screws. But the ships still would be known for their pitch and roll, a result of their narrow beams — rough seas were tough on tender stomachs.

During the makeover, an enclosed observation salon was built on the gallery deck forward and a veranda café-ballroom on B deck aft. Decorator panels between the windows featured painted figures representing the "Spirit of Carnival." The salon was to be the focal point of shipboard social life during the day, including service as a reading room. At night, oriental rugs were rolled aside and the area became a cabaret with a buffet and music for dancing.

Some of the old deluxe suites were combined for greater comfort, leaving twenty-six on each ship. Redecorated in pastel colors, they were renumbered (but with no Number 13). Some were furnished with brass beds, as in the original décor. Bachelor rooms with single beds and

THE CHESTER COMPASS

A NEWSPAPER DEVOTED TO   INTERESTS OF EMPLOYEES

MERCHANT SHIPBUILDING CORPORATION
"THE SHIPYARD WITH A TRADITION"

| Vol. 3 | CHESTER, PA., JULY 1921 | No. 9 |

THE S. S. YALE BUILT AT THE CHESTER SHIPYARD AND RECONDITIONED AFTER UNUSUAL SERVICE

Photo by courtesy of S. Pomeroy Trood, Los Angeles Shipbuilding and Drydock Co.
Los Angeles, California

THE YALE like its sister ship, Harvard, was launched from this yard in 1907.   After fourteen years of hard service without being laid up for repairs, the Yale and Harvard were recently reconditioned, and are now in service of the Los Angeles Steamship Company, California.

The Yale and Harvard are triple propeller passenger liners and can maintain an average maximum speed of 25.8 knots.   Both crafts were decorated by the Government for meditorius service as troop transports in the World War.

Although reconstruction took place on the west coast, the Merchant Shipbuilding Corporation at Chester, Pennsylvania, successors to the John Roach Company, thought it newsworthy enough to put on the cover of their company publication. Author's collection

showers were installed on the boat deck. Deluxe suites were abaft of the observation room. Each ship was remodeled to accommodate 480 passengers, compared with the pre-war 896. Facilities included a barbershop, beauty salon and valet services.

Cargo space on both ships was enlarged to handle 1,000 tons of freight and for the first time some passengers could take their automobiles along (by 1934 the total was 1,061 cars for the year). Once again the *Yale* and *Harvard* firerooms were fully converted to oil and a Coen oil-burning system installed. When the restored ships underwent trials, the *Yale* achieved a speed of 24.6 knots, making her the fastest ship on the Pacific Coast. (The *Harvard* was close on her heels at 24 knots flat and later set a company record with a southbound run from San Francisco's Mile Rock to Point Fermin, San Pedro, in 16 hours, 34 minutes, averaging 21.1 knots for the 347 miles.) The *Yale* also was the first ship on the Pacific Coast equipped with a radio loudspeaker so passengers could hear broadcasts from pioneer shore stations (a ship newspaper, with mimeographed news bulletins, also was offered).

The final touch was to replace the hulls' Navy gray paint (which had taken over from the "dazzle" color scheme) with the original color that had made the White Flyers so distinctive — at an extra annual cost of $4,000 over a darker hue. Now the ships were described as the "White Comets" (there was another company whose name was White Flyer Line). To top off the new-old look, each ship's stacks were painted the original black, except that the forward stack now bore two gold chevrons as a mark of the sisters' wartime service (similar to the overseas service chevrons worn on the lower left sleeve of Army uniforms of the period).

While the ship restoration was going on, arrangements for the new line progressed ashore. The prewar facilities on Terminal Island no longer were available, so plans were made for the ships to tie up at Berths 155 and 156, Pier A, in Wilmington, farther up channel. "Boat trains" — four

Because of the existence of White Flyer Line, the ships were referred to as the "White Comets." The courtesy card, left, was issued to an employee of Southern Pacific to allow him free passage. Bill Stritzel Collection

Fully dressed, the Yale *pulls away from her pier in Wilmington on her first postwar voyage as part of the LASSCO Line on May 2, 1921. Steamship Historical Society of America, Everett E. Viez collection*

or five big red cars of the Pacific Electric regional service — would form up at the central station at Fifth and Main Streets in downtown Los Angeles about an hour before sailing time to transport passengers and baggage direct to dockside. Similar arrangements were made from the Ocean Avenue station in Long Beach. In the San Francisco Bay area, Southern Pacific "red trains" and the orange Key System units provided transport on the eastern shore to the bay ferries that brought passengers to the Embarcadero where LASSCO's terminal was at Pier 7, not far from the Ferry Building.

May 2, 1921 —

At last express service along California's rugged coastline was ready to resume. The *Yale* would operate alone at first, since work on the *Harvard* was slowed by labor difficulties and other problems. Port and line officials planned a gala sendoff, with the cooperation of the Navy, now making the outer harbor at San Pedro its main Pacific Fleet anchorage. The *Yale* was fully dressed for the occasion and carried a near-capacity passenger list. Several hundred guests of LASSCO lunched aboard and were serenaded by the ship's orchestra, set up on the top deck.

A large crowd was on the dock to witness the departure, and supplies of paper serpentine and confetti were distributed to passengers with which to pelt the well-wishers. The Los Angeles High School Boys Band, aboard a nearby ferryboat, added to the musical program. (LASSCO officials learned that day that the serpentine and confetti gave a glamorous touch to *Yale/Harvard* sailings at little expense — the "paper snowstorm" henceforth became a standard event at each sailing.)

The *Yale*'s 3 p.m. departure on May 2, 1921 began slowly down the San Pedro Channel (a four-MPH speed limit was required by harbor officials in the narrow waterway). While cheers and music echoed from ship to shore and back, the White Flyer was accompanied by a flotilla of civilian craft and units of the Navy. To honor both the *Yale* and the *Harvard* for their wartime service, a destroyer — possibly USS *O'Bannon* (DD-170) — and two submarine chasers, *No. 298* and *No. 306*, escorted the

At first the Yale *made the coastwise run alone. Here she is shown underway on San Francisco Bay. Many of the photographs of this era show the chevrons on the forward funnel (installed to honor the ships' war service) darkened. Whether this was for artistic or political reasons is unknown. San Francisco Maritime National Historical Park, Mrs. M.L. Pittel Photographic Collection*

Yale to sea. In the outer harbor, battleships and other major vessels of the fleet saluted her with sirens, foghorns and ships' whistles while bands played and sailors cheered from the decks. It was a glorious beginning as the White Flyer (or "Comet") churned away to the northwest up the Santa Barbara Channel.

May 3, 1921 —

Harbor vessels sent out blasts of their horns and whistles to greet *Yale* on her arrival in San Francisco Bay — two hours late. Stiff headwinds that sent waves washing over her bow had forced her to slow down. But a large crowd greeted her happily at Pier 7, along with civic dignitaries, chamber of commerce officials and shipping line magnates. The ship's crew was busy making everything shipshape for a fast turnaround — the *Yale* sailed that afternoon on the southbound leg, right on schedule.

August 5, 1921 —

The *Yale* operated alone for three months, maintaining a schedule of two round trips a week except for one nine-day interruption caused by a labor dispute. Now the *Harvard* was ready to rejoin her sister. Like that of the *Yale*, the *Harvard*'s initial voyage was hailed by ships and community leaders at both harbors. Reporter S. Fred Hogue of the *Los Angeles Times* described the morning arrival at San Francisco as being greeted by "a steady staccato of fog signals, steamer whistles and other noise."

The Harvard *joined her sister after a few months and overnight coastwise service between San Francisco and Los Angeles was established once more. Note the darkened chevrons on the steamers forward funnel and the battleship in the background. San Francisco Maritime National Historical Park, A.E. Wells Photographic Collection*

The Los Angeles Steamship Company offered "The Overnight Trip De Luxe on the Finest and Fastest Coastwise Steamships." Note the attempt to go head-to-head against the Matson Navigation Company on service to Hawaii, upper right. The Steamship Historical Society Of America, J. Mack Gamble collection

Hogue waxed poetic, describing the *Harvard* as

> … floating serenely across the Golden Gate like a great white swan … Moonlight and the sea. Maidens will do well to travel on the *Harvard* with their hearts kept under lock and key. And wise husbands will not send pretty wives on too many of these excursions alone. For the great white swan never goes sailing without a Lohengrin on board.

Thus early on was established the postwar reputations of the White Flyers as romantic vessels, where shorebound cares could be forgotten once the lines were cast off. A night at sea was a time for romance or adventure, before the return of reality at the dock after breakfast. This was the Roaring Twenties (Prohibition was observed in the breach, much as it was ashore). The Terrible Thirties were almost a decade away.

The *Yale* and the *Harvard* now began alternating service with five sailings a week from each port, leaving at 3 p.m. from Los Angeles and arriving at San Francisco at about 9 a.m. the next morning, departing on the southbound run a few hours later. While the runs were like those of the pre-war days, the fares were nearly doubled. Passage ranged from $18 to $25 in a two-berth stateroom to $32.50 to $50 for deluxe quarters. These figures were later reduced to meet competition (especially from highway buses) and as boom times switched dramatically into the era of the Great Depression. (An example: a round trip fare in 1930 cost $10 with four meals and two nights' lodging.)

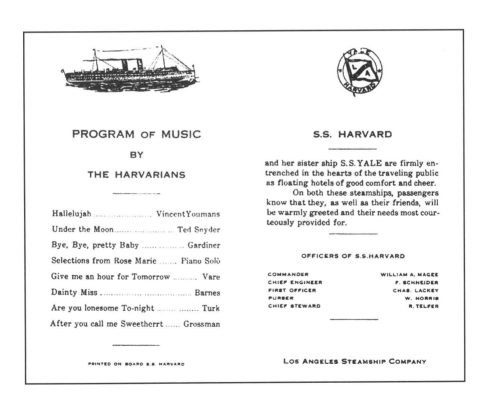

Promotional items given to passengers included a listing of the officers and the music program offered by the ship's band, the "Harvarians." The Huntington Library

With the addition of San Diego at the southern end of the route came a new brochure highlighting the attractions of the ships and their destinations in California's three major ports. San Francisco Maritime National Historical Park

June 22, 1922 —

San Diego had been part of the swift sisters' service area prior to the war. Now leaders of the LASSCO Line were ready to call again. Sailings of each ship had been cut to four a week, making a loop down the coast to San Diego an easy fit. The border city was a popular destination in those days (liquor was available just over the border in Mexico and a resort atmosphere existed there). City and company officials were aboard the *Yale* when she sailed south from Wilmington at 3 p.m. June 22, 1922, on the initial voyage.

About 300 persons were on hand to greet the ship at San Diego's Municipal Pier at the end of the five-hour trip. It was *Yale*'s first visit in five years. After a formal reception, the ship was thrown open for dancing. More than 12,000 persons boarded for the gala event.

The San Diego run grew in popularity. LASSCO increased the service to two visits a week in November, 1922; to three in April, 1924, and finally to four in 1925.

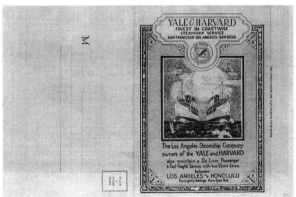

One of the more popular items on board was this mailer, complete with menu and photos of interiors, that could be sent through the purser's office to friends ashore. Author's collection

While the *Yale* and *Harvard* grew in popularity, the LASSCO leadership had to devote much effort to marketing the service, as well as the other ships the company had purchased for the run to Hawaii. H.F. Alexander's Pacific Steamship Company (Admiral Line) served all of the major Pacific Coast ports and provided stiff competition. But the "White Comets" quickly took the bulk of the California trade. One of the most successful marketing efforts was a slogan contest in 1921. LASSCO offered a $500 prize for the slogan best fitting the sister ships. More than 150,000 entries were received from all over the country. The winning slogan was "Royal Trips on Regal Ships." (Never mind what that had to do with the collegiate twins from the Ivy League.)

Part of the success was LASSCO's ability to attract the college crowd bound for athletic events in the San Francisco or Los Angeles areas, especially the big football games of the Twenties and Thirties. Supporters

The same format as on the previous page was used for charters and large groups attending conventions, such as the Southern California Exchange Clubs. The Huntington Library

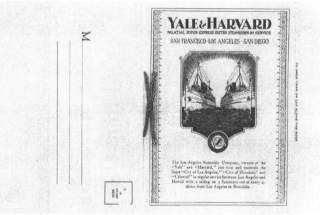

ALONG THE CALIFORNIA COAST

The handsome billboard on the highway said: "Between San Francisco and L.A.Take the *Yale* and *Harvard* Way. It's the restful, pepful, overnight trip deluxe."…Learning that the "*Yale* and *Harvard* Way" was distinctly the popular way to Los Angeles, we boarded the *Yale* one fine afternoon, Jack finding that all he had to do with his car was to "just drive it aboard" about half an hour before sailing time.

Mother and Dad had a deluxe stateroom on the upper deck — twin beds, private bath and all the appointments and luxury of a high class hotel ashore. Jack and I had a "standard" stateroom … with all the comforts we had enjoyed when we went to Europe last year on one of the biggest of the Ocean liners …

On the dot of the sailing hour we were off; down through the shipping of the harbor and out to the open sea through the Golden Gate, that most impressive of harbor entrances … We strolled up and down the great promenade deck, watching the shoreline with the Cliff House and beaches slide by, until a bellboy appeared, announcing to the accompaniment of a musical gong the welcome news that dinner would be ready in half an hour.

With sharpened appetites we enjoyed an excellent dinner, admirably served at a private table in the great dining salon … We again strolled the deck … then were attracted to the veranda café ballroom by the announcement of dancing. This proved indeed a fascinating feature of the trip. The ballroom is in the stern on the upper deck. The music is supplied by the ship's orchestra and the superb dancing floor is surrounded by cozy, cushioned nooks with little tables at which light refreshments are served those who wish to sit and be entertained by the music and dancing within, as well as by the beauty of the "moon upon the waters" seen through the windows.

After a most refreshing night's rest and a good breakfast, Mother went to the restful and sun-bathed ladies' lounge and writing room; Dad found a splendidly appointed barber shop and a smoking room that was particularly attractive, and a few of us prevailed on the orchestra to give us "just one after-breakfast trot." Then we all went on deck to watch far-famed Catalina Island and our approach to Los Angeles Harbor as we rounded the breakwater lighthouse and passed through a most imposing array of Uncle Sam's battleships moored inside.

Steaming past stretches of busy dock and warehouses of the inner harbor we came to our dock of debarkation alongside which a special boat train of electric cars was standing to take passengers to Los Angeles, Long Beach, Pasadena, etc.

As easily as he had driven it aboard, Jack drove his machine onto the dock and we were away once more … determined also to persuade all our California-bound friends … to see that they are routed "the *Yale* and *Harvard* Way" between San Francisco and Los Angeles.

—LASSCO marketing brochure, mid-'20s

YALE AND HARVARD		
Twin Palaces of the Pacific		

INCLUDING BERTH AND MEALS	1st Class—One Way Fares	
	Between San Francisco and Los Angeles, Wilmington or Long Beach	Between San Francisco and San Diego

DECK	ACCOMMODATIONS	FARE	FARE
A	Bachelor Suites with Single Bed, Private Shower-bath and Toilet	$25.00	$32.00
	Suites De Luxe with Double or Twin Beds, Private Shower Bath and Toilet	25.00	32.00
B	Outside Two Berth Staterooms—Amidship	22.00	26.50
	Outside Two Berth Staterooms—Aft	21.00	25.50
	Inside Single and Two Berth Staterooms	19.00	23.50
C	Outside Two Berth Staterooms	20.00	24.50
	Inside Single and Two Berth Staterooms	17.00	21.50
CHILDREN'S FARES			
	2 Years and under 5 Years	3.50	4.50
	5 Years and under 12 Years	Half Fare	Half Fare
	Under 2 Years - - -	Free	Free

Between LOS ANGELES LONG BEACH or WILMINGTON and SAN DIEGO	First-Class, One Way Fare Including Dinner Southbound or Lunch Northbound	$4.50

ROUND TRIP FARES Including Meals and Berth
Return Limit 16 Days

Between SAN FRANCISCO and LOS ANGELES WILMINGTON or LONG BEACH	**$25.00**
Between SAN FRANCISCO and SAN DIEGO	**$31.00**
Between LOS ANGELES WILMINGTON or LONG BEACH and SAN DIEGO	**$6.00** Including Dinner Southbound and Lunch Northbound

ROUND TRIP TICKETS WITH LONGER LIMITS AT SLIGHTLY HIGHER FARES

Corrected to March 20, 1927

The prices in 1927 were competitive but the Great Depression was just over the horizon and they would soon plummet. Author's collection

of the state's major colleges and universities were actively wooed as soon as game schedules were announced (at San Francisco, some Saturday afternoon sailings were delayed until 1 a.m. Sunday so passengers could enjoy post-game festivities). High school excursions also were popular, especially between Los Angeles and San Diego, with contingents bound for the games accompanied by bands to provide musical support. Older groups were not ignored — marketing efforts were directed at lodges, clubs and civic organizations, providing special programs while transporting delegates to state and national conventions. The idea was to make the north-south trip between California's major population centers a pleasurable experience — and LASSCO succeeded. On at least one occasion the line went out of its way to provide a public service. After rains washed out roads and railroad tracks between Los Angeles and San Diego in February, 1927, LASSCO chartered the Catalina Island steamer *Avalon* from the Wilmington Transportation Company to operate beween the two cities. The *Avalon* made two trips before the special service ended.

October 4, 1930 —

The remaining years of the Roaring Twenties were successful ones for the *Yale* and the *Harvard*, but increasing economic difficulties in Pacific maritime affairs, climaxed by the stock market crash of 1929 that signaled future trouble ahead, brought a "morning after" sense of reality to the line's operators. By 1930 LASSCO faced serious competition on its Hawaiian service (the company now had twelve ships). Its biggest challenger, the Matson Navigation Company, with more than double the

This postcard (note the LASSCO insignia in upper right) depicts the second City of Honolulu *in earlier days. Her appearance is similar to the* Harvard *and the* Yale. *Author's collection*

The City of Honolulu *burned at her pier in Honolulu on May 25, 1930 and was scuttled to avoid an explosion of her cargo of nitrate. Steamship Historical Society, University of Baltimore Library*

The City of Los Angeles, *center, is shown berthed in San Francisco in May, 1934. The three nearest freighters were American-Hawaiian ships. Embarcadero real estate was utilitarian in the Thirties.* San Francisco Chronicle

vessels, was getting bigger. LASSCO ships were aging and required big expenditures for replacements — the line at one time operated such noted former German transatlantic liners as the *Friederich Der Grosse* (built in 1896) and the *Grosser Kurfurst* (1900). The former, renamed the *City of Honolulu*, caught fire on the return leg of her maiden voyage to Hawaii in October, 1922, and sank after all 217 persons aboard were rescued (a second *City of Honolulu* also was a total loss by fire, in Honolulu in May, 1930). The *Grosser Kurfurst* became the *City of Los Angeles* until finally scrapped in 1937.

Rumors of a merger had circulated in July, but were denied. Terms of a merger were agreed upon on October 4, 1930, but not revealed until three weeks later. Under the agreement, LASSCO would continue to operate the California service, but as a subsidiary of Matson (Ralph Chandler became a Matson vice-president, still running LASSCO). For all intents and purposes, operations would continue unchanged, although Matson's leadership would direct the future course of the "White Comets."

But even those plans would not stand for long.

LASSCO's commitment to its Hawaii service is clearly shown by this poster depicting the Calawaii *sailing in the Territory of Hawaii. Bill Stritzel Collection*

10

HARVARD
HITS HONDA

Memorial Day weekend in 1931 was a busy time for the fast turbiners, now operating as integrated units of the Matson Line even though still maintaining the LASSCO Line's public identity. The observance of the holiday honoring the nation's military dead, successor to what originally was called Decoration Day after the Civil War, was May 30, which fell on a Saturday that year. Many events were planned at the LASSCO ports of San Francisco, Los Angeles and San Diego around the date.

As they had for so many years on both coasts, the *Harvard* and the *Yale* made almost simultaneous departures the afternoon of Friday, May 29, the latter on a northbound run from the Wilmington dock and the former from San Francisco's Embarcadero and out through the Golden Gate. For the *Harvard*, it was her 972nd California voyage. Sadly, it would be her last.

Sometime during the night between Point Sur and Point Arguello, the two ships passed near each other on opposing northwest-southeast courses. It had happened hundreds of times before, but this passage was different. Capt. Frank A. Johnson, veteran master of the *Yale*, noted the *Harvard* passing him a half-mile inshore, more than 2½ miles inside her normal southbound route, on a line that ultimately would take her onto the rocky coastline. But Capt. Lyle B. Hillsinger was no stranger to the perils of the Central California coast (he had been in command of the *Harvard* since April, 1929, and had many years' experience before that). Captain Johnson said nothing to Captain Hillsinger at the time — one veteran ship commander must assume another of like experience knows what he is doing.

The dangers of California's shore were known to mariners the world over. From San Francisco Bay to San Pedro, the rugged coastline offers little shelter from Pacific storms and currents pushed by winds blowing from the north and west over vast reaches of open sea. The state's distinctive angled shape also requires navigators to first keep clear, then adjust their southeastern course to turn more easterly south of the coastline's "elbow" to enter the Santa Barbara Channel in the twenty-three-mile-wide gap between Point Conception and San Miguel Island. The "elbow" is Point Arguello, central feature of a stretch of coast long known as a graveyard of ships.

So remote is the rugged land east and north of Point Arguello that even today no highways reach the area. An outcropping on Arguello's northern face is Point Pedernales, and the adjacent land feature is a mesa and canyon known since early Spanish days as Honda. It still is just a dot on most maps, a maintenance site on the Southern Pacific (now Union Pacific) rail line cut along the jagged coast of the Santa Ynez Mountains deep within the confines of Vandenberg Air Force Base.

Since the Gold Rush more than fifty vessels had grounded on the jutting coastline. The most noteworthy wrecks were the steamer *Yankee Blade* in 1854, with a loss of twenty lives and $153,000 in gold bullion; the famous coastwise passenger liner *Santa Rosa*, a 1911 grounding in which four died; seven U.S. Navy ships of Destroyer Squadron 11 which steamed onto the rocks just south of Point Pedernales in a heavy fog the night of Sept. 8, 1923 — and the White Flyer *Harvard*, which came flashing ashore at 19½ knots in the early hours of May 30, 1931, almost within a mile of the Navy wreck site. (The spot now is marked on maps by a shoreline feature known as Destroyer Rock.)

Twenty-three sailors died when the seven destroyers — half the fourteen steaming in column to San Diego in a 20-knot cruising test — pounded ashore in follow-the-leader fashion. It was the Navy's worst peacetime disaster. Luckily, no lives were lost aboard the *Harvard*, but the ship was a total loss and the San Francisco-Los Angeles "overnight boat" service never again was the same.

There were many similarities in the events leading to the two disasters. Faulty navigational assumptions, dead-reckoning errors and distrust of the technology of the time were a few. But the irresistible force of nature — a strong eastward current — was the principal cause in both cases.

By the Twenties, Point Arguello not only boasted a powerful lighthouse but also a Navy-manned radio direction finder (RDF) station (then called a radio compass station). Using a loop antenna, the RDF operator ashore could focus on an incoming radio signal to pinpoint the compass bearing of the sender, an aid to ships' navigators. The drawback was that the operator of the loop antenna had to know, within 180 degrees, where the sender was. It was the failure of the ship to recognize its position far to the east of the normal route that resulted in disaster.

The *Yale*'s captain was not the only one to notice *Harvard*'s deviation from her normal course that night, perhaps resulting from an undetected extreme southeasterly "set" or drift of current insidiously pushing the ship shoreward. Farther south at the Point Arguello Navy Direction Finder Station, close by the Point Arguello Light, Radioman 1/c E.M. Barnes, who had thirteen months' experience at the station, also was disturbed by the bearings he was reading on *Harvard*'s radio signals. She was churning southward far inside her usual route — so much so that he once sent the ship a reciprocal southerly compass reading, in case the liner had somehow gotten below the point, into the Santa Barbara Channel. *Harvard*'s radio operator quickly advised Barnes "We R N" (We are North).

The usual party-like atmosphere that typified weekend voyages aboard the White Flyers had settled down after midnight — only a few of *Harvard*'s 497 passengers were still up. This shipload may have been more staid than most — about half of those aboard were returning home to Los Angeles and San Diego from the annual meeting of the California Congress of Parents and Teachers, just concluded in San Francisco. Stewards and ship's officers had to quiet a noisy private group or two, but most passengers were in their cabins for the night.

Captain Hillsinger also had retired to his cabin. His standing night orders to the duty officer read "Steer 130 degrees. Watch steering carefully. Call me within 10 miles of Point Arguello."

Second Officer George P. McVicar was in charge on the bridge as the *Harvard* speeded toward her destiny at 19½ knots. The night was mostly fogless, but haze obscured the shoreline. The ship's first communication with the Direction Finder Station came at 2:53 a.m. when the liner asked for a bearing. Radioman Barnes sent a reading of 335 degrees. He was concerned because this was well to the right (from his viewpoint) or inshore of the bearing usually furnished to the fast turbiners at this time of the morning in accordance with their scheduled runs. On the next bearing request, at 3:10, the *Harvard* was so far to the right of the usual mark that he did not believe the ship could be to the north, so he gave the southerly reading, 172 degrees. The *Harvard*'s operator promptly replied, "We are up the other way." A third bearing, this time a northerly 352, was sent and acknowledged by the ship at 3:17. Barnes, now clearly worried, wrote down a message he intended to send as part of the next contact: "Your note (signal) five degrees broad but you are very close to beach."

Barnes never got to send it — the next word from *Harvard* came at 3:26 a.m.: "SOS. Ashore at Point Arguello NW." The actual spot later was determined to be Lat. 34° 36' 50" North, Long. 120° 38' 25" West, 1,150 feet off shore and 2.3 miles north of the Point Arguello Light. It is at Honda, about a mile from Point Pedernales, where the seven destroyers drove aground. Both tragedies resulted from disbelief in the competence of the Radio Direction Finder staff and the accuracy of the bearings.

On the bridge of the *Harvard*, Second Officer McVicar, confused by the bearing reports, had used valuable time as he consulted with the ship's radio officer. They both assumed an inexperienced operator was sending the bearings, the first of which indicated the ship was nine degrees "inside" Point Arguello and the second twenty-six degrees "inside." When McVicar called Captain Hillsinger to the bridge at 3:07 a.m. he failed to apprise him of the seriousness of the situation, leading Hillsinger to believe he had more time to deal with the problem.

Hillsinger ordered a ten-degree right turn to seaward, then switched on the fathometer to check the ocean depth. But the fathometer needed time to warm up before it gave readings. As the captain began to realize the ship's dire situation he gave the command, "Clear Over!" Almost simultaneously, *Harvard* ground onto the sandbars and rocks that extend out from shore in stratified lines. It was only after the impact that McVicar saw the Point Arguello Light through the inshore haze.

(In testimony before a Steamboat Inspection Service board of inquiry, McVicar blamed himself for the crash by taking too long to call the captain. In the lost ten minutes, "I could have held her up, stopped the ship," he testified. The captain told investigators he assumed the

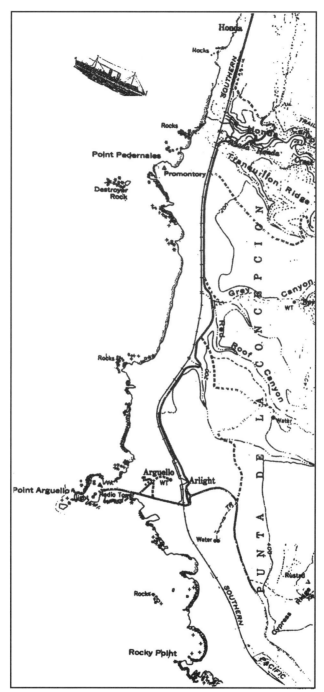

Map shows approximate spot where the Harvard *drove aground. For scale, distance from Point Arguello to Point Pedernales is two miles. Author*

"twenty-six degrees inside" report had just been received and that he had ample time to correct the course.)

The best news that morning for Captain Hillsinger was that the weather was almost perfect and the ocean flat calm except for the regular swells rolling in. The *Harvard* drove so far onto the rocks and sand that she was almost on an even keel when she jolted to a sudden stop. There was no panic as awakened passengers found the liner steady and still when they were quickly ordered into lifeboats (Hillsinger, afraid of the rocky coastline, directed the boats to keep off the shore while awaiting seaborne help. No time was wasted however — many of the passengers were still in their nightclothes, wrapped in coats and blankets, when taken aboard rescue ships. But as Hillsinger was to report by radio later in the morning, "All passengers kept their shirts on" and "nobody even got wet feet.")

Help already was on the way in the busy north-south ship channel. After *Harvard*'s first SOS at 3:26 a.m. at least six ships turned in her direction — the freighters *San Anselmo* and *Marsodak*, en route to San Francisco; three Coast Guard cutters, and the Navy's brand new cruiser USS *Louisville* (CA-28) in the Santa Barbara Channel. Even the *Yale*, nearing San Francisco, gave thought to turning about to charge to the rescue of her sister White Flyer, but it immediately became clear other vessels were much closer. A relief train even was assembled in Santa Barbara and made ready to steam north with doctors and nurses to stand by near Honda in the event the boats brought the victims ashore. Residents

The cruiser USS Louisville *(CA-28) was on her first trial runs when the distress call came in. She quickly responded. This photo was taken from USS* Wasp *circa 1940-41. U.S. Naval Historical Center Photograph*

The Harvard*'s lower deck is under water in this aerial view of the stern taken shortly after she grounded near Point Arguello. The rescue ships* San Anselmo *and USS* Louisville *are in the background. This photo probably was taken from the press plane piloted by Col. Roscoe Turner. San Francsico Maritime National Historical Park*

of Honda, Surf, Arlight, Arguello and Lompoc gathered on the rocky bluffs to offer assistance, but could only watch the drama unfolding offshore.

The Quaker Line's World War I-vintage intercoastal freighter *San Anselmo*, en route from San Pedro to Oakland, was late to learn of the mishap but first on the scene. She found most of the passengers and a large part of the crew bobbing on the calm surface of the Pacific in high spirits, singing and joking as they awaited rescue. It was pure chance that the *San Anselmo* got there first. "At about 4:30 Saturday morning I was approaching Point Arguello and I wasn't sure of my position," said Capt. A.N. Wennerlund. "So I awakened my radio operator, Warren Peters, and told him to get me a radio position. He intercepted the *Harvard*'s distress messages and we immediately put on full speed (twelve knots) and ran to her assistance. If there were no fog and I was sure of where I was, the radio operator would have slept and I probably would have learned of the accident after we reached port."

The *San Anselmo* reached the wreck site at 7:15 a.m. and anchored three-quarters of a mile from the *Harvard* in eleven fathoms of water. Within ten minutes the freighter crew was taking the passengers aboard from the boats.

Captain Wennerlund described his operation for the *San Francisco Chronicle* after his ship arrived at Oakland: "I broke out the cook. I knew if anybody was to be rescued they would be hungry and cold, and nothing makes things seem better than a cup of hot coffee and something in a man's belly. We were all ready for them.

"It was very foggy when we came alongside of the *Harvard* and we had a hard time finding her. But we finally located her boats, and took aboard everybody in them. There were only eight men in the boats. The rest of the 200 were women and kids — I never saw so many kids in my life.

"There were kids all over my ship. Never in my life have I seen a braver or finer bunch of women than those passengers. There was no panic, no hurry, no mistake. But there was plenty of laughter as they came up the ladder. And half of them only in their nighties and pajamas, too! The old *San Anselmo* got a real treat!

"Thacker, the cook, made gallons and gallons of coffee, and he was right there at the rail, handing a steaming cup to each woman as she came aboard. Later, he made soup and toast for all hands. They certainly lit into it, all right! ... The most

Passengers from the Harvard, *all properly hatted, male and female, disembark from one of the lifeboats alongside one of the rescue vessels. They left their lifejackets in the boat. San Francisco Maritime National Historical Park Photographic Collection*

popular man on my ship was Thacker the cook. He's the best cook in the Pacific."

The freighter captain described how he introduced a woman, an avowed "dry," to her first taste of alcohol. "She was little, middle-aged, dressed only in her coat and nightdress, sick, cold and a bit hysterical. I offered her a slug of whiskey and she said, 'Sir, I am a prohibitionist and liquor has never touched my lips.' I poured a slug into her anyway, and she seemed to like it."

He also told of the passenger who said she was eighty years old and on her first sea voyage. "She had cut her leg somehow and asked me to bandage it for her, and I took her into my cabin and did so. 'Now, lady, you can lie down on my bunk for a while,' I said. 'Well, I should say not,' she came back. 'I wouldn't miss seeing everything for worlds. It's great fun,' and she hobbled out on deck to watch the rest of the passengers come aboard."

Shortly after the *San Anselmo* started taking on the passengers, the *Marsodak* and the USS *Louisville* arrived. Since her help was not needed, the *Marsodak* soon was released to proceed on her journey. After a conference among the captains, it was decided the *Harvard*'s complement would be trans-shipped to the cruiser and the Navy would take responsibility for carrying the victims to port. (The *San Anselmo* would transport fourteen of *Harvard*'s eighteen lifeboats to Oakland.)

The 10,000-ton, eight-inch-gunned cruiser USS *Louisville* would provide a special chapter in the unexpected sea saga the *Harvard* passengers would have to pass on to their families and friends on arriving home. Commissioned only the previous January, the ship was still in her acceptance trials when the *Harvard*'s call for assistance came crackling over the airwaves. *Louisville* was headed for San Pedro, completing a two-hour fifteen-knot fuel-economy test thirty-seven miles west of Point San Vicente. Since the cruiser had been testing at various speeds, all her boilers were still hot; the ship immediately turned about and was surging north at over thirty knots within a half-hour.

The *Louisville* reached the shipwreck scene at 7:25 a.m., only a few moments after the two freighters. The cruiser anchored at 7:53 and put over her rescue boats. Preparations already had been made to receive the shipwreck victims. Bunks in certain spaces were set aside for civilian use, blankets and clothing were collected and cooks had prepared hot soup, coffee, tea and food. The cruiser's motor launches proceeded to round up the *Harvard*'s lifeboats and transfer passengers already aboard the *San Anselmo* to the Navy ship. The *Harvard*'s purser, Thomas Keating, supervised the recovery of valuables from the ship's safe and passengers' baggage by the cruiser's launches, along with the rest of the non-essential crew. Only the *Harvard*'s deck force and engineers remained aboard — it was hoped that somehow they would be able to refloat the ship at high tide if the hull was not too badly damaged.

At 10:10 a.m. the Coast Guard cutter *Tamaroa* arrived to assist the stricken liner and by 11:20 a.m. all those requiring rescue were aboard USS *Louisville* — a total of 575 men, women and children, the 497 passengers and the remainder from the crew (the overall number aboard *Harvard* was listed at 622). Capt. E.J. Marquart, commander of the cruiser who had assumed control at the scene, released the *San Anselmo* to proceed to San Francisco Bay, while the cruiser turned south for San Pedro at 11:33, cranking up to twenty-five knots. Most of the hand luggage had been placed under guard aboard the cruiser, but some of the items were loose. Noted Capt. Marquart: "The luggage included even a dog and a canary bird, also ladies' shoes and various articles of apparel, apparently once loosely wrapped in newspapers by hands helpful to salvage. It was evident that some passengers had not exchanged night clothes for underthings before embarking in the life boats."

The cruiser was in radio contact with Adm. J.V. Chase, commander in chief of the Navy's Battle Force, and the headquarters of the 11th and

Fortunately for rescue operations the Harvard *grounded on a day when the ocean was flat calm. This photo probably is from the press plane piloted by Col. Roscoe Turner.*
San Francisco Maritime National Historical Park Phtographic Collection

12th Naval Districts in San Diego and San Francisco, advising them of the rescue operation with sparse details for the news organizations. Now the ship was the recipient of dozens of inquiring messages sent from shore by relatives and friends, not to mention all the major news agencies. An early news source was Col. Roscoe Turner, the internationally famous speed pilot, who flew a plane bearing photographers to the scene and gave the first eye-witness account upon their return to Los Angeles.

"A heavy fog was just lifting when we circled the *Harvard* about 10 a.m.," said Turner. "We flew around for about fifteen minutes to get the pictures. At times we got within fifty feet of the sea — some of the boys wanted to find out if they could see the officers' stripes. They could... The ocean was very calm and the sea about the *Louisville*, where they were taking the passengers, was dotted with lifeboats. It was a bit chilly and you could see the passengers wrapped in coats and blankets.

"When they saw us they waved and shouted cheerfully ... We looked around for a landing place, but the country was too rough, so we flew back over the ships again, waggled our wings and went home." The bulk of the stories would have to await the rescue ship's arrival in Los Angeles harbor. Here are a few:

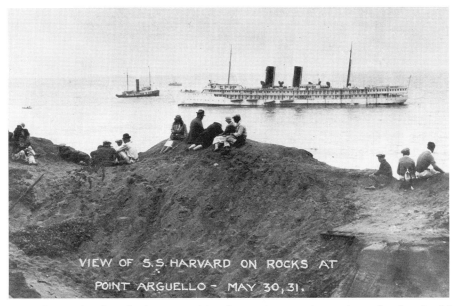

A small crowd gathered ashore, watching the rescue operation and standing by, should they be needed on the desolate stretch of coastline. San Francisco Maritime National Historical Park John W. Procter Photographic Collection

—Georgiana Turnbull of San Francisco said she was reading in bed when the ship struck. "I felt a slight jar and then a bounce. I wasn't afraid, so I didn't get up. Fifteen minutes later I got up. There was no fog when I went on deck. I could clearly see the shore and the lights of a railroad train. When we boarded the cruiser *Louisville* I heard a man say 'I was petrified when I saw that drunken seaman carrying that baby.' Personally, I saw no intoxicated person. There was no confusion when the lifeboats were lowered. I had the distinction of being the last woman to leave the *Harvard*."

In southern California, the Los Angeles Evening Herald *put out a special edition to cover the event and the* San Diego Union *devoted the entire front page to the* Harvard *grounding. In the northern part of the state, The* San Francisco Call-Bulletin, *an afternoon newspaper, ran extra editions to get news of the incident to an eager public, while the* San Francisco Chronicle *featured it on the front page the next morning.*

The Los Angeles Examiner *Sunday coverage ran to three pages, which is understandable considering the number of "hometown" passengers on board.*

—The youngest passenger, seven-month-old Lois Ann Akers, daughter of George Akers of Oakland, spent two hours in a lifeboat without a whimper. Florence Gernandt, age two, daughter of Mr. and Mrs. Fred J. Gernandt of Oakland, thought it was part of the lark of being on a big boat when her father lowered her into her mother's arms in a small lifeboat. Probably the oldest aboard was another Oaklander, Mrs. Elizabeth Stoddard, eighty-two, who had been looking forward to an ocean voyage for years.

"It was a shipwreck de luxe" in the view of Mrs. Stoddard. "No one was hurt—it was a genuine thrill and it earned us a ride on the Navy's newest cruiser."

—The beautiful lady in the silk boudoir robe used only one hand while descending a ladder into one of the *Harvard*'s lifeboats. Another woman passenger thought it was modesty, based on fear her robe would blow open. But when she sat down, the woman opened her other arm and released a tiny Pomeranian, who jumped out, shook itself, and barked. "That was the funniest episode of the wreck," said Mrs. C.H. Caldwell of Del Paso Heights, Sacramento.

The aftermath of a quick, but orderly ship abandonment — empty davits, open doors, the decks littered with chairs, blankets and miscellaneous pieces of equipment. The horizon shows the ship was on an even keel. San Francisco Maritime National Historical Park San Francisco Call-Bulletin *Photographic Collection*

—"I was never so happy in my life as when the *Louisville* picked us up," said Nathan L. Fairbairn of San Francisco. "We got in the boats, shook hands with acquaintances we had made Friday night and never expected to see each other again. The reports would have you believe it was all play, but my hands are all cut up from trying to hold boats together, and my back still aches."

—Another dog, "Rowdy," owned by Naomi Soule of San Francisco, was being transported in the *Harvard*'s carpenter shop. When the evacuation was ordered the carpenter turned the dog loose. Many passengers then put aside their own safety concerns of the moment to dash about the ship in pursuit of Rowdy. Not until her pet was back under control would Miss Soule enter a lifeboat.

—While awaiting lowering of lifeboats after daybreak, someone suggested to a ship's officer that the orchestra should play some tunes. Mustered on deck, the musicians cut loose with "Goodbye Forever", followed perhaps more appropriately with "How Dry I Am".

—Albert D. Everett of Lompoc and Myron Douglas of Los Angeles, along with three children, were on the bluffs at Honda at 4 a.m. on their way to search among the rocks for abalone at a super low tide. "We were on the cliff, just starting down," said Everett, "when all of a sudden we heard whistles start screaming…. We could just see a dim shape through the mist, and then we saw lights begin to flash out—it must have been when the passengers were awakened and began turning on their cabin lights.

"We scrambled down to the beach and started using our flashlights on the chance that somebody on the ship might see them. Evidently they did because the ship's blinker light began flashing in our direction, apparently trying to send a message, but of course we couldn't read it.

"Pretty soon a boat cut out from the ship and got within about twenty yards of shore, but couldn't make it. He (someone in the boat) told us what had happened…and the boat went back to the ship"

—Dixie, the pet canary, owed her rescue to a marine serving aboard the cruiser. Her owner, Mrs. Nannie Loveless of Washington, D.C., left the canary aboard the *Harvard* during the passenger evacuation. When the woman told the sailors of her abandoned bird, a boat was dispatched to bring the canary to her. Dixie was well-traveled — Mrs. Loveless said she had taken the canary on trips covering more than 16,000 miles. The shipwreck must have been a new experience, however. The bird had not sung a note since the wreck.

—Seaman 1/c Art Martin, on the *Louisville*, hoped to be assigned to assist the rescued passengers, but instead was ordered to search the luggage for contraband liquor. Martin recalled later that several bottles did turn up (Prohibition was still in effect) and were confiscated. Perhaps this explains the need for the guard.

—One of the first persons on the *Louisville* to greet Mrs. James B. Willy of San Diego and her seventeen-month-old daughter, Caroline, was Navy Lieut. Ralph Hickock, a luncheon guest in her home only a month before, when he announced he was reporting to the cruiser. "As a lifeboat from the *Louisville* approached the *Harvard*, I thought I recognized the officer in charge," Mrs. Willy wired her parents. "In the excitement, however, I lost the thought. A few moments later I was shaking hands with Lieutenant Hickock."

—Not all of the passengers had good things to say about the *Harvard*'s crew. There were reports of drunkenness among the lifeboat crews after the grounding, but Captain Wennerlund of the *San Anselmo* said the liner's men "pulled in good sailor fashion and made good landings alongside."

Captain Marquart's report to the Secretary of the Navy and the Chief of Naval Operations detailed the *Louisville*'s southbound trip. As is routine aboard naval ships, the mess hall had been decked out with special table decorations and bunting for the Memorial Day meal — at first mistakenly assumed by some of the rescued as having been laid on in their honor. Said Marquart: "A turkey holiday dinner … was augmented by chicken, etc., so that all rescued fared exceedingly well at the noonday meal."

Describing the atmosphere aboard his ship, the skipper said the rescued not only consumed the regular rations, but also "ice cream, candies, post cards, etc., from the ship's store pleased many. Bunks in certain assigned compartments afforded sleeping places for those desiring, and the sick bay, with its staff, took care of the few inclined to invalidism or shock effects. Radio broadcasting programs entertained, also visiting parties about the ship…"

By 6 p.m. the *Louisville* had cleared the San Pedro breakwater and in little more than thirty minutes was anchored in the fleet anchorage. Three minesweepers — the USS *Brant*, the USS *Tern* and the USS *Alcorma* — quickly moved alongside to transport the rescued to the LASSCO dock in the inner harbor at Wilmington. The last passengers and luggage left the *Louisville* at 8:53 p.m.

A tumultuous scene greeted the rescued at the dock as friends and newsmen crowded about while the wreck victims tried to sort out the mixed-up luggage before proceeding to their destinations. But the

With one tug alongside to starboard and two standing by the Harvard *awaits salvage assessment and the decision as to whether or not she will sail again. Author's collection*

efficiency and kindness of the Navy was not forgotten. The gentleness of the sailors to the women, some of whom were upset, was recalled by Mrs. Caldwell. "I never knew men could be so kind and gentle," she said, her voice breaking. Other Southern California PTA officials wrote to the Secretary of the Navy to make sure he knew of the "excellent manner in which our delegates were taken care of by the U.S. cruiser *Louisville*." Similar sentiments were voiced in a commendation resolution adopted by the Downtown Association of San Francisco.

In his report to his superiors, Captain Marquart concluded by commending various members of his crew and added, "the general and very complete preparations … to meet every contingency ensured a safe and rapid embarkation of the rescued before unfavorable weather could set in, and ample comfort and attention for the shipwrecked.

"Had the sea not been smooth, or had bad fog set in, one must shudder at the probable terrible cost in life on that rockbound and exposed section of the coast."

How correct he was would be proved within a matter of hours.

S.S. "HARVARD" IN THE PRIDE OF LIFE,
AND IN THE THROES OF DEATH, OFF POINT ARGUELLO

In July, 1931, the Fireman's Fund Insurance Company included a history of the Harvard, *emphasizing the disaster, in their publication,* Fireman's Fund Record. *The above collage served to illustrate the piece. Fireman's Fund Insurance Company*

11

THE

PERFECT WRECK

In the first moments after the *Harvard* skidded to a sudden stop on the rocky outcropping at Honda, Capt. Lyle B. Hillsinger ordered the forward hold to be flooded, to keep the liner firmly in place. He knew the benign weather and sea conditions would not last — Point Arguello's history was all bad in that respect.

After the evacuation of the passengers in the ship's lifeboats had been arranged, and the rescue ships arrived, the deck force and engineers could concentrate on efforts to save the liner. Despite hopeful statements from General Manager Ralph Chandler and other LASSCO officials in Wilmington, a check of the hull's condition by those still aboard indicated it would be a daunting task.

The departure of the *San Anselmo* and USS *Louisville* left only the Coast Guard cutter *Tamaroa* on the scene, ready to rescue the remaining crewmen if necessary. The *Tamaroa*'s arrival had provoked a bit of humor in an otherwise grim picture. The cutter was on a ten-day patrol out of San Diego and had anchored in the lee of San Nicolas Island to chip and paint her tall stack with red lead. Since the vessel had originally been a seagoing tug, her freshly painted stack made her appear to be one of the line of Red Stack tugboats out of San Francisco Bay. LASSCO had already arranged for salvage assistance from San Pedro, the *Tamaroa* was

Within a few days the wreck began to break up as shown by this photo taken early in June, 1931. Soon there would be nothing above water. San Francisco Chronicle

told, "We don't need you — no one ordered a Red Stack tug. The Coast Guard is coming. Go away!"

"This IS the Coast Guard," was the reply.

Company officials had quickly organized a force to salvage the million-dollar "White Comet" from her perilous perch, if it were at all possible. Three tugs were immediately dispatched from San Pedro. But as soon as Ralph Gardner, an expert from the salvage firm of Merritt-

---

A SEALED REPORT

George Hillsinger, son of the captain of the *Harvard* and a Southern California trial lawyer, visited the wreck site for the first time in 1976 and told a reporter stories his father had related to him, then age six, about the event.

The elder Hillsinger said one of the mates wanted to try to back off the rocks, but "I told him it would rip the bottom of the ship off and we'd all go down." Said the son: "I remember my father telling me that the only casualty was an unfortunate woman passenger who was bitten on the behind by a seal while attempting to board a lifeboat." There is no official verification of this mishap, sealed or otherwise. The story may have grown out of a news report that a woman passenger had been bitten on the hand by a "friendly" seal during the evacuation.

Chapman & Scott, reached the scene early Sunday morning, May 31, it was almost certain the *Harvard* would be a total loss.

Gardner's assessment, wired from the tug *Peacock*, dismayed company officials: "Condition of *Harvard* very serious. She will not stand any bad weather. All holds appear punctured except hold aft of collision bulkhead. About five feet of water over main deck aft and one foot forward. We are now boating the cargo to the tugs and will make pump tests as soon as possible."

The other tugs were the *Homer* and the *Commissioner*. The liner carried 350 tons of cargo worth more than $260,000 but how much would be accessible for removal depended on the weather. Salvors were quoted as saying it would take at least a week before any effort could be made to float or drag the liner off the rocks, a forlorn hope as it turned out.

The *Peacock*'s crew installed a gasoline hoist with three six-inch, one twelve-inch and one ten-inch pump in various compartments, a difficult task because the *Harvard* was laid out principally for passenger accommodations. It was necessary to burn out bulkheads, chop down elaborate fittings and do other damage to place the pumps most effectively. The locations made it doubtful the gear could be removed in time if the ship broke up. (They did manage to do so, however.)

By Wednesday, June 3, heavy seas and wind forced the salvage tugs to cast off their lines and seek shelter in Santa Barbara Bay, the *Homer* carrying sixty-five tons of the liner's cargo and twenty-one members of the crew to San Pedro. The waves battered the *Harvard*'s hulk so severely that Captain Hillsinger and the few officers with him went aboard the cutter *Tamaroa*, later to return home. The salvage crews were to formally abandon the ship and strike her colors the next day, June 4, as salvage master Gardner could only send word that "heavy seas continue."

Capt. John Johnson of Norfolk, Virginia, another expert called by the salvage firm, arrived at Santa Barbara the night of June 4 and reached the wreck the next morning. The details of his examination were reported in *Steamboat Bill*, publication of the Steamship Historical Society of America (Winter, 1960):

> The *Harvard* was laying broadside to the beach very low in the water. The big seas rolling in would at times break in on top of C-Deck. (Salvage Officer Gardner) informed me that the *Harvard* was going to pieces and was past saving. Salvage operations had been abandoned and the work recovering our gear had to be suspended owing to rough seas … On arrival on board the wreck we made an examination. The vessel was full of water all over. The

heavy sea was breaking over C-Deck and into the vessel. She was working continuously with the sea. The vessel would roll and strike from bilge to bilge … Her superstructure would also work the same as the hull. One part would move one way and the other would move the other way according to the surges.

Johnson said he observed a crack in the shell plating about four inches wide on the port side at the D-Deck line and extending down into the water, about midway between the foremast and the forward smokestack. He added: "All the superstructure had been broken and started by the seas breaking over the vessel and by the working of the hull.

"She was a perfect wreck."

A similar assessment came from David Young, chief surveyor for the Board of Marine Underwriters in San Francisco. "Not much hope," he wired the board after a visit to the wreck. He described the vessel as "pitching and rolling heavily" as a rising north wind sent billows crashing into the hull.

By 7 a.m. June 5 it was clear the *Harvard* was breaking up. The salvage workers concentrated on removing their gear, and what portion of *Harvard*'s equipment they could. Splits in the hull had widened under the pounding of the sea — one was plainly visible to the hundreds of spectators on the bluffs about 1,200 feet away.

Even though it was clear not much would be saved from the ship, her sale to Merritt-Chapman & Scott for $1,000 was announced on June 7, "as is, where is." The salvage firm expected to recover its costs. But six days later, watchers on shore got the last glimpse of the "White Comet," her bow gone and sagging to her starboard side, as she slid off her rocky perch and disappeared into deep water between the rocks. The *Harvard*, one of the sister White Flyers, was gone after an exciting quarter-century. Underwriters paid out $1.5 million for the ship and an additional $250,000 for the cargo.

(Wreckage from the wooden parts of the ship washed ashore on the rocky coast for weeks. Residents of Lompoc and the smaller communities retrieved much of the lumber and other flotsam, including barrels of coconut — still edible until one tired of it. Today, only a few relics of the ship are to be found in the museum of the Lompoc Valley Historical Society.)

A federal inquiry by the Steamboat Inspection Service of the U.S. Department of Commerce (predecessor to the U.S. Coast Guard in these matters) began almost as soon as the wreck survivors arrived on shore. Every passenger who had testimony to offer, good or bad, was questioned

For weeks after the Harvard *sank local beachcombers went through the wreckage that washed up on shore. Note barrel at upper left. Lompoc Valley Historical Society*

by Capt. Samuel Kennedy and J.A. Moody, U.S. steamboat inspectors in Los Angeles. Survivors who returned quickly to Northern California (some took the train, but some sailed back on the *Yale*) were questioned in San Francisco and the information sent south. The *Harvard* officers, including Captain Hillsinger, testified before Captain Kennedy in Los Angeles.

There were a few extraneous issues, such as isolated incidents of drunkenness among stewards and some other crew members after the crash and testimony that an erroneous course bearing was deliberately placed in the ship's log. But the focus of the investigation centered on the conduct of the two officers on the bridge at the time of the crash — the captain and Second Officer George McVicar.

Testimony revealed that there was a strong "set" by the currents to shoreward just before the crash and that the captain was unable to see the Point Arguello Light when he reached the bridge. "Do you believe," asked Kennedy, "that if you had been in the shoes of your second officer when he received the second radio bearing from Point Arguello stating that you were twenty-six degrees starboard of Point Arguello that you could and should have saved the ship?"

"Unquestionably," said Hillsinger.

But he "firmly but courteously" refused to place the blame for the crash on the shoulders of any of his officers. (It was during these sessions that McVicar, questioned by Moody, declared that he had not acted quickly enough because of his confusion over the bearing reports from the Point Arguello radio station.)

On June 17 charges of "negligence and unskillfullness" were preferred against McVicar and "unskillfullness and inattention to duty" against Captain Hillsinger. Third Mate Oscar S. Anderson was charged with falsification of records for entering an incorrect course bearing in the ship's log. All pleaded innocent in brief hearings before Kennedy, but all were found guilty.

Captain Hillsinger lost his master's license for four months. He subsequently became a port pilot for the Los Angeles Harbor Department before and after service in the Navy in World War II. He retired at age 70 and died in 1970.

For the most serious offense, McVicar's license was suspended for one year. Anderson's infraction resulted in a fifteen-day license suspension.

LASSCO attempted to maintain the quality and efficiency of the overnight service by a temporary substitution of its steamer *Calawaii* (built in 1893 as the British liner *Mobile*), followed by the Clyde liner *Iroquois*,

Without her running mate, the Yale *tried to continue the service as shown by this ticket envelope noting the connecting Pacific Electric Railway train. The Huntington Library*

The Yale *continued with three round trips a week between San Francisco and Los Angeles with a swing south to San Diego once a week. Here the* Yale *is shown on San Francisco Bay in 1931. San Francisco Maritime National Historical Park Procter Photographic Collection*

leased from the Atlantic Coast for six months at $1,000 a day. The *Iroquois*, built in 1927, had good passenger accommodations and a garage for eighty cars, but could not match the *Yale*'s speed. The old schedule of the twin "White Flyers" could not be maintained, so the costly arrangement was terminated at year end. (The *Iroquois* gained fame as the hospital ship *Solace* in World War II.)

Shown in 1927 when new, the Iroquois *ran on the east coast for the Clyde Line. She later came out to California to run with the* Yale. Moran Tow Line

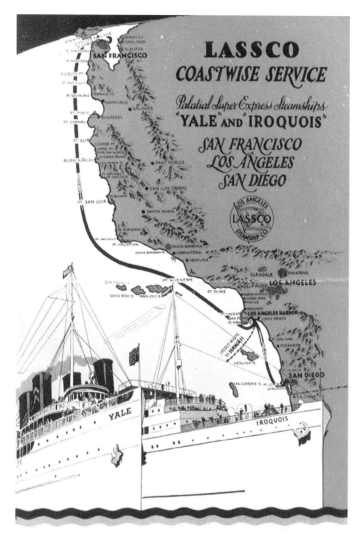

With the Iroquois *came a new brochure advertising LASSCO's continued coastwise service. Bill Stritzel Collection*

12

THE
LONE COMET

The Yale would carry on alone, generally making three round trips a week (one to San Diego), for nearly five more years before a combination of economic conditions — declining passenger counts, increasing costs, growing competition from land transportation, and labor strife beyond her control — spelled the end of the "overnight boats," leaving behind a collage of shipboard memories in their wake. With both vessels having been gone for more than a half-century, it has become difficult to find passengers who sailed aboard the fast turbiners. But those who did never forgot the experience:

Broken Streamers, Spinning Logs

Jack Whitmeyer of Long Beach made two trips, both southbound from San Francisco, as a young boy. "I remember a summer trip in 1929, I was about eight years old. We lived in San Francisco, and my mother didn't like to ride the train. We sailed at 4 p.m., and between the Golden Gate and the Farallones it was rough, but the crew was really 'pouring on the coal', if I can use that expression.

"I was interested in everything about the ship. I learned then what a taffrail log (a device to measure speed in the water) was—I saw

125

The LASSCO Coastwise Log

SAN DIEGO
LOS ANGELES
SAN FRANCISCO

S. S. YALE, AT SEA.

GEORGE H. ZEH, U.S.N.R. COMMANDER.

SEPTEMBER
TUESDAY,
SEPT 29,
1 9 3 1.

(Furnished through courtesy of Associated Press and Mackay Radio).

WASHINGTON :: Administrations program for economy in government as a
result of constantly mounting deficit is going to hit U. S. Navy hard-
est of all departments, it is said.Numbers of destroyers to be built
will be halved and modernization of battleships also will be abandoned
in one of most stringent moves ever undertaken by the government to
save money. If all these economics are effected, United States will be
in position of being virtually on naval holiday and will probably drop
to third position among naval powers of world with Great Britain first
and Japan second in standing.

-----0-----

WASHINGTON :: QUESTION of Prohibition was treated again at Washington
when 'enry Syevens, newly elected president of American Legion, denied
charge by Clarence True Wilson of Board of Temperance, that Detroit
convention of legion was "drunken orgy". There was another echo of
Detroit when Representative Patman declared he will introduce bill in
Congress for cash payment of bonus despite adverse vote of legion,
which, he said,"traded bonus for beer". Mr Patman also said he will
fight for impeachment of Andrew Mellon.

-----0-----

DENVER COLORADO :: Despite protest of aged prelates who expressed fear
that teachings of Christ were being taken lightly, House of Bishops of
Episcopal Church voted to change canon law on remarriage of divorced
persons. Change in effect makes it possible for divorced persons to
obtain from specially elected church courts declaration that original
marriage was null, thereby making remarriage possible for them within
the Episcopal church. Clergy and lay deputies are expected to approve
change in substance so that it will become Episcopal Church law.

-----0-----

PHILADELPHIA :: Eight bank failures were reported in United States
Monday. The largest institution was Northern Central Trust Company of
Philadelphia which had deposits of more than three million dollars.

-----0-----

NEW YORK :: Discovery of pair of tennis shoes which Mrs Benjamin Coll-
ings said were worn by one of pirates who killed her husband, provided
what Suffolk County officials considered important clue to murder mystery. Ownership of shoes has been partially traced, it was said.

-----0-----

GENEVA :: Disarmament committee of League of Nations failed to reach
agreement on kind of armament truce which might be brought into effect
amo ng nations, and committee adjourned after offering question to sub-
committee.

-----0-----

OTTAWA :: Canadian government decided to admit British goods to country at par value of British pound. Owing to depreciated condition of
currency this action amounts to 14 percent preference.

*The ship's paper included news of concern to travelers of the day: the devastating
effects of the Great Depression were felt throughout the country, the Prohibition question
was hotly argued, items from foreign capitals were included. The daily LASSCO
Coastwise Log was produced by the purser's office with the radio operator supplying
the substance of the news reports. The Huntington Library*

the line twirling and saw the seaman bringing in the impeller. I guess it was used for dead-reckoning (navigation).

Dance music was provided on board for those so inclined. Author's collection

"There was dancing for older couples back then, but that didn't interest me much. The next morning we got to Wilmington at 10 a.m. and stayed aboard until the *Harvard* came in from San Diego. My father had a 16-millimeter Kodak camera and he shot film of the other ship. I remember watching stevedores using hand trucks to load cargo and supplies. I recall them using hand trucks to load orange crates.

"As the ships prepared to sail, a band was playing and passengers threw streamers (serpentine) — hundreds of them — down on to the crowd on the pier. As an eight-year-old I was concerned when they all broke as the ship backed away. Then we sailed out of the harbor, past San Pedro and continued south. I remember coming in around Point Loma and we could see all the lights. We sailed up San Diego Bay and landed at the Broadway pier."

A significant memory of a young passenger after more than seventy years is "the food was very nice."

In addition to standard fare, the breakfast menu, left, included salt cod and lamb kidneys. The chrome badge, above, was worn by either table waiters or room stewards. Left, author's collection, above, Bill Stritzel collection

Like a Train On a Track

Bill Olesen of San Pedro was twenty-seven when he made a round trip on the *Yale* in 1933. He was on business in the San Francisco area. His father was marine superintendent for a lumber firm, so Olesen had a background associated with coastal shipping.

With the Yale *sailing alone, LASSCO had to produce a new brochure, reflecting its coastwise service. The Huntington Library*

"I had a cabin to myself and the ship served an excellent dinner," recalled Olesen. "It was a beautiful night and the sea was calm. "We slashed along like a train on a track — you'd look back at the wake and it was straight as a die.

"They had slots (machines) on the ship. They had an orchestra playing for dancing. The ship also was serving drinks (this was after Prohibition was repealed). Breakfast was served off Monterey and by

On Board S. S. Yale

FRANK A. JOHNSON, U.S.N.R. COMMANDER
Tuesday, July 5, 1932.

Dinner

Canape au Tuna

Queen and Ripe Olives   Celery en Branche

Cream of Spinach   Consomme, Tapioca

Poached Red Snapper, Lobster Sauce

Boiled Shoulder of Lamb, Caper Sauce

Hungarian Goulash with Spatzen

Corn Fritters, Hot Maple Syrup

Broiled Squab Chicken a'la Espagnole

Roast Prime Ribs of Beef au jus

Browned Potatoes   Boiled Potatoes

Saute of Tomatoes   Braised Onions

SALAD

Lettuce & Egg Salad

A BIT OF SWEET MAKES THE MEAL COMPLETE

Steamed Suet Pudding, Cinnamon Sauce

Petit Fours

Neapolitan Ice Cream   Assorted Cakes

American and Swiss Cheese

Bent's Toasted Crackers

Milk, Tea and Coffee

Dinner on the Yale *included a cross-section of popular American cuisine: Hungarian ghoulash and shoulder of lamb vied with prime rib and squab chicken for the diner's attention. The Huntington Library.*

Bill Olesen might well have had his breakfast eggs in the two-egg cup, left, and his morning toast in the bread tray above. Note the LASSCO emblem on both. Bill Stritzel Collection

the time we arrived in San Francisco at about 9 a.m. we were ready to go ashore and get down to business.

"After a while you could recognize the whistles of different ships — some were 'triple-toned', discordant. The *Yale* and the *Harvard* had single-tone whistles, but the depth of tone, or pitch, made each distinctive.

"I remember as we moved north we overtook several small steam lumber schooners. One was close aboard, rocking along at about eight knots. We passed her like she was standing still."

Olesen summed up his memories of the last of the "White Comets": "It was strictly first class — no attempt at skimping. It was the most luxurious experience I ever had."

Pasadena!! All Aboard

Excerpt from the *Liscum News*, publication of the E.H. Liscum Camp No.7, United Spanish War Veterans, Oakland, Calif.; March, 1934:

"Once more Southern California is calling to the comrades and sisters of the department to assemble in the Sunny South. This year the

Illustration from the mailer given to passengers. Author's collection

Department Encampment will be held in Pasadena…Memories of several wonderful trips to encampments…on the Steamer YALE have prompted many comrades to request that another trip by steamer be organized. Therefore, arrangements have been made for the reservation of a large number of rooms on the S.S. YALE… for the use of the United Spanish War Veterans….

"The luxury and harmony of the fittings and furnishings of the YALE are well known to the comrades of the U.S.W.V. They know every nook and corner of the large public spaces, social halls and lobbies and they are familiar with all the delightful spots up "topside" where they can enjoy the bracing sea breeze and the health-giving sunshine.

"The favorite gathering place for the U.S.W.V. will be the Veranda Café Ballroom. Here an excellent ship's orchestra holds forth every evening for those who enjoy dancing. Arrangements have been made to have this orchestra play the old timers the United Spanish War Veterans love so well: "A Hot Time in the Old Town," "Banks of the Wabash," "The Sidewalks of New York," and many other hits of '98. A number of special features are being arranged which should add interest to the trip…."

Bouquets For the *Yale*

Clara Ostoich, a longtime San Pedro businesswoman, has a special place in her heart for the *Harvard* and *Yale*. As the operator of a flower shop in the coastal community from 1928 to 1945, she remembers delivering "truckloads of bon voyage bouquets" to the fast turbiners.

But her memories of the two ships go deeper, especially for the *Yale*, to a sailing in 1925 when as a seventeen-year-old girl she made a trip alone on the "White Comet." The highlight, she recalls, was dinner at the captain's table.

"I don't know to this day why I was selected," mused Mrs. Ostoich. "I remember as I came aboard I was handed an envelope containing an invitation requesting my presence at the captain's table. I was thrilled — there was one other officer seated at the round table, along with about four passengers." Her alert mind is filled with a lifetime of memories, but she no longer recalls the subjects of dinner conversation. Even so, visions of that sailing from Wilmington to San Francisco have stayed with her forever. Perhaps the captain felt a need to offer protection to a seventeen-year-old traveling alone? Mrs. Ostoich got no indication, but admits, "I was pretty good looking."

After starting her flower shop at Sixth Street and Pacific Avenue, Mrs. Ostoich had many orders for floral displays at events in the San Pedro area, but personally made all the deliveries to the passenger ships, ordered by wire from across the nation. "It was fun to go on the ships," she remembers. "The port officials and the stevedores all knew me and passed me right through. And the officers of the ships always treated me special."

She never sailed on the white flyers again. She has a photo taken on that 1925 trip, but not aboard the *Yale*. She had made the voyage to visit a sister on a chicken ranch in Petaluma. The picture shows a young lady just off a swank coastal liner — surrounded by a field of hungry chickens.

~~~

The longshoremen's Pacific Coast waterfront strike of 1934, which tied up all shipping for three months and resulted in a general strike in San Francisco and labor strife in all major ports, was a harbinger of maritime troubles to come (another prolonged waterfront strike would occur in 1936). On Oct. 1, 1935, for the first time in her west coast career, the operators of *Yale* withdrew her from service for the winter. By then the fast turbiner had made 1,330 trips since 1921, covering 1,270,000 miles. *Yale*'s voyages were restarted on May 17, 1936, but almost immediately it was evident the service could not be maintained. "Continuously advancing operating costs have made the service

After being laid up for the winter of 1935-1936, the Yale *was prepared for coastwise service once again. When this photo was taken on May 12, 1936, she was being painted prior to resuming service five days later. San Francisco Maritime National Historical Park John W. Procter Photographic Collection*

Another view of the Yale *on May 12, 1936, as she receives a fresh coat of paint prior to resuming coastwise service. Unfortunately, the once-popular ship's return was not to last. San Francisco Maritime National Historical Park*

unremunerative," said J.E. Ryan, the general passenger agent in San Francisco.

Without fanfare, the *Yale* sailed north from Los Angeles for the last time on July 5 and after reaching San Francisco the next morning was moved up the bay to a lonely dock in an isolated backwater at Antioch. It appeared the spot was just a temporary stop on her way to a breaker's yard.

But the saga of the fast turbiners had one chapter still to be written.

The Yale *in lay-up at Antioch, California, circa 1940-1941. Located in the upper reaches of the Sacramento River delta, this area has the advantage of relatively fresh water, an effective deterrent to corrosion in steel hulls. Jack Whitmeyer*

PART V

WORLD WAR II

13

SEA DOG DAYS
IN ALASKA

The *Yale* spent five years tied to her Antioch pier while time passed her by. The United States emerged from the Great Depression. The rest of the globe moved inexorably toward a second World War. Maritime operating conditions led to the tieup of six more Matson ships in waters adjacent to the White Flyer (no longer an apt description as her exterior paint deteriorated and rust stains became her main decoration). Gradually the other vessels were sold off to foreign shipping interests until the *Yale* was alone once more.

When war threatened again a way was found to regenerate the aging fast turbiner for another round of service. In March, 1941, Matson sold the *Yale* for $24,000 to the Seims-Drake Puget Sound Company, contractors on naval projects, for use as a floating hotel in Alaska. (Actually, the purchasers were the Seims-Spokane Company; Johnson, Drake & Pieper, and the Puget Sound Bridge & Dredging Company, each holding a third interest.)

Towed from her longtime backwater location, the *Yale* was delivered to the Moore Dry Dock Company yard in the Oakland Estuary, where she was lifted out of the water to have her hull scraped and repainted. Barnacles, seaweed and grass hung from her three propellers, rudder and hull. Her decks were warped and cracked and thick layers of dust coated her superstructure and interiors. Moore yard workers gave her "a shave and a haircut," as they called it; refurbished her engineering spaces and equipment and overhauled her machinery. After nine days and with a minimum crew, she departed on March 22 for Sitka, Alaska, where her new owners were building facilities for the Navy. Later, the ship was moved to Kodiak, continuing her role as a dormitory ship for 600 construction workers and as a mess hall for 1,200. But once more the Navy was to find a higher duty call for the old speedster.

Inter-island transport was deemed inadequate in the Aleutian chain and the Navy decided the old *Yale*, part of the famed "Channel Express" in World War I, was the answer (although how her narrow hull might react in stormy sub-arctic waters apparently was not considered). She was taken over by the Navy on April 30, 1943. A team of twenty Seabees began the task of refitting the old White Flyer, which had been sitting in the mud. Lieut. (j.g.) Edwin B. Heath, who had shipfitting training, took charge, assisted by Ensigns James Grow and Gratan C. Boomer, with machinists' backgrounds, and Paul M. Hunt, who had deck experience.

Taken in 1937, this aerial view of the Moore Dry Dock Company shows where the Yale *was towed to prepare her for World War II service. Within six years Moore would expand from 4,000 workers to 37,000.* The Story Of Moore Dry Dock Company

COAST LINER YALE SAILS PACIFIC IN SECOND WAR

SAN FRANCISCO, Dec. 19. (*P*) The veteran coastal passenger vessel, the S.S. Yale, is sailing the Pacific in her second war after being a beached bunkhouse for Alaskan construction workers, the 12th Naval District disclosed today.

Temporarily lifting the censorship rule that prohibits the use of ships' names in newspaper stories, the Navy said that the former Los Angeles Steamship Co. liner has been recommissioned for convoy service.

The Navy explained the Yale had weathered two winters of outer Alaska storms while serving as a stationary hotel and that "she was too gallant a ship to die that way."

Comdr. C. P. Nash, U.S.N.R., former American-Hawaiian Line master, has been assigned to the one-time San Francisco-Los Angeles vessel and says "the old girl is just as good as new."

The Yale*'s return to service rated this article in the* Los Angeles Times, *December 20, 1943 and similar articles in the* San Francisco Chronicle. *Author's collection*

Within thirty days they had the *Yale* reconditioned enough to be delivered to the Puget Sound Navy Yard in Bremerton, Washington. After general reconditioning — and a complete repainting in Navy gray — the ship was commissioned on August 8, 1943, with Lt. Cmdr. W.N. VanDenbrugh in command. It had been the *Harvard*'s fate to be renamed in the first big war; now it was the *Yale*'s turn. On August 19 the ship was renamed USS *Greyhound* (IX-106). The reason for the name change in the ship's second war was not noted, nor why it was not appropriate to name her Bulldog after her Yale University antecedents. But at least the

Taken on July 30, 1943, this photo shows the Yale *at Kodiak, Alaska, as she appeared after serving as a hotel for Siems-Drake Puget Sound Company. National Archives*

By September 10, 1943, the Yale *had been moved to Dutch Harbor, Alaska, and was being prepared for Navy service as USS* Greyhound *(IX-106). Although painted over, the raised letters Y-A-L-E can be seen on the bow, above. Note the laundry hanging between the rafts on the upper deck in photo below. National Archives*

name chosen was one associated with speed (even though the ship only hit fifteen knots in her shakedown cruise).

Then USS *Greyhound* was returned to Alaskan waters, shuttling between various Aleutian ports, centering on Dutch Harbor. But perhaps her officers found her unsuited for ferry service in northern latitudes — early in 1944 she was returned to Puget Sound and, on March 31, was decommissioned. Her service to the Navy continued for four more years as a floating barracks, first for the Ship Repair Unit at the Bremerton yard, and then for personnel at various training schools. During this period she had a complement of five officers, eight petty officers and 155 enlisted men. The *Greyhound*'s last assignment was as flagship for the Commander, Bremerton Group, Inactive Fleet. She finally was placed out of service on March 9, 1948, and stricken from the Navy List on June 18.

There seemed no further role for the old sea dog USS *Greyhound*. She was turned over to the U.S. Maritime Commission and placed with other ships of the National Defense Reserve Fleet at Olympia, Washington, on November 12, 1948. The following June she was sold. The contract required that she be "completely scrapped, dismembered, dismantled or destroyed, within the confines…of the United States."

The steam tug Hercules *as she appeared during her long active career.* The Story Of Moore Dry Dock Company

The successful bidder was the Walter W. Johnson Company, which maintained a dismantling yard in Stockton, California. This meant *Greyhound* — still fondly remembered as the *Yale* — would pay one final visit to San Francisco Bay. At mid-afternoon on July 20, 1949, the old White Flyer, wearing a coat of Navy gray now symbolic of her age, moved in through the Golden Gate at the end of a cable hauled by the Red Stack tug *Hercules* after a seven-day trip from Puget Sound. She still sported two white chevrons on her forward funnel, proud service stripes of her World War I duty in the English Channel. No one was aboard her and there was no fanfare, but many San

Franciscans noted her passing. (Among them was Mrs. J.C. Geiger, wife of the city's health director. She was the daughter of Charles W. Morse, the Bath entrepreneur who had ordered the *Yale* and *Harvard* built more than forty-two years before.)

Off Treasure Island, the *Hercules* dropped the tow and three river tugs nuzzled up to the hull. It was the job of the Bay Cities Transportation Company to steer the old *Yale* to her final destination at Stockton. The job was directed by Walter Westman, Bay Cities general manager. He knew the *Yale* well — many years before he had sailed on her on his honeymoon.

It was fitting that on her final voyage the old fast turbiner was accompanied by a friend.

PART VI

EPILOGUE

14

WHISTLING DOWNWIND IN CHICAGO

The saga of the *Yale* and the *Harvard*, encompassing more than four decades, two major wars, two oceans and two of the nation's coastlines, comes to an end, of all places, in the country's heartland, far from the sea. This postscript results from the whim of yet another national figure, Col. Robert R. McCormick, powerful publisher of the *Chicago Tribune*. The good news is that a significant relic of the ships survives to this day, even though far removed from familiar waters — the *Yale*'s steam whistle.

(The folklore surrounding the fast turbiners includes a whistle story about the *Harvard*, as well. Frank O. Braynard, in his *Famous American Ships*, tells of an unidentified rancher at Point Arguello in 1931, hearing the sound of a ship's whistle, noting something familiar. He recognized it as the distinctive tone of the *Santa Rosa*, a total loss on the point twenty years before. The rancher had a good ear, declared Braynard — the *Harvard* was sounding distress calls from her auxiliary whistle, salvaged from the *Santa Rosa* in 1911 and later installed on the *Harvard*'s after stack.)

The *Yale*, nudged up the Stockton ship channel by the Bay Cities tugs, reached the Walter W. Johnson yard in a few hours from San Francisco Bay, but work on her demolition did not start until July 25, 1949.

Company workers put in 2,320 man-hours on the job, with the *Yale*'s scrap metals sent by rail to the Columbia Steel Company's mill at Pittsburg, California. (The breakup was halted during the month of October by a strike at the steel plant.)

The work was completed on December 17. The hull and other recoverable parts of the White Flyer, assembled by expert hands in construction yards in Chester, Pennsylvania; Hoboken, New Jersey, and Los Angeles, produced 2,532 tons of steel scrap, forty-one tons of lead, eight tons of copper, eighty-four tons of brass and two-and-a-half tons of babbitt, an anti-friction alloy.

But the breaker crews saved her whistle.

While Walter W. Johnson was a friend of McCormick, his "official" reason for giving the whistle to the nationally known newspaper publisher went unrecorded. Perhaps it was because McCormick was a Yale University alumnus, or perhaps McCormick, who served in the 1st Infantry Division in France during World War I, crossed the English Channel on one of the *Yale*'s many voyages as a troopship. In any event, McCormick had an important use for the relic.

The story of the whistle is told in an article by author A.J. Liebling in *The New Yorker* magazine (Jan. 7, 1950). McCormick had the 200-pound brass whistle, four feet high and ten inches inches in di-

One item to survive the scrapping of the Yale *is this room key. Bill Stritzel collection*

ameter, shipped to Chicago where he was constructing an atomic-raid alarm system and shelter in the *Tribune* building, one of Chicago's distinctive business structures. (Even today, the Tribune Tower, incorporating in its white "business gothic" walls pieces from Westminster Abbey, Notre Dame Cathedral and the Taj Mahal, is noteworthy — in the colonel's words, "the most beautiful commercial building in the world (and) workshop of the world's greatest newspaper.")

In 1950 McCormick was much concerned about the possibility of an atomic attack, so he took steps to protect his employees. After workers tested the *Yale*'s whistle in the newspaper's machine shop using only ninety pounds of compressed air (it emitted an "earsplitting sound," was the report), the whistle was installed on the seventh-story roof. At the

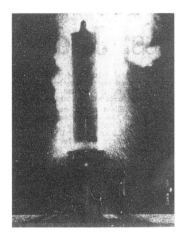

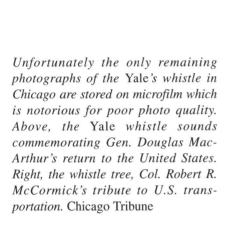

Unfortunately the only remaining photographs of the Yale*'s whistle in Chicago are stored on microfilm which is notorious for poor photo quality. Above, the* Yale *whistle sounds commemorating Gen. Douglas MacArthur's return to the United States. Right, the whistle tree, Col. Robert R. McCormick's tribute to U.S. transportation.* Chicago Tribune

same time, the colonel had stored specially made rolls of newsprint paper ready to stack in the halls of the building to provide a bomb shelter of sorts in the event of an enemy attack.

Luckily, those under the protection of the *Chicago Tribune* never had to rely on newsprint rolls to ward off the blast or radiation effects of an atomic bomb. The only time the *Yale* whistle ever sent its wails echoing through the urban corridors of downtown Chicago was on April 16, 1951, to announce Gen. Douglas MacArthur's arrival in the United States after President Harry S. Truman fired him from his post as supreme commander in the Far East.

In 1954 the *Yale*'s whistle was taken from the roof and incorporated into a "whistle tree" with six other historic whistles McCormick had collected — from the sidewheel packet *Robert E. Lee*, the armored cruiser

USS *Seattle*, the Tribune pulpwood carrier *Shelter Bay*, the Chicago fire-boat *Geyser*, the New York Central's speedy locomotive, No. 999, and Chicago fire engine No. 11. They became an exhibit in a Tribune Tower museum. Most of the museum's collection, including the whistle tree, was turned over to the Chicago Historical Society after McCormick's death in 1955. Although not on display, the *Yale*'s whistle, along with the others, is still a part of the society's collection.

Except for the whistle and a ship model in the San Diego Maritime Museum, little remains of the *Yale* and the *Harvard* except for photographs, business records, marketing brochures and a few items of memorabilia. It is ironic that although the *Harvard* lived only about half as long as the *Yale*, more of her can be found — at Honda.

The hull is said to be a popular hangout for the fish.

ABOUT THE AUTHOR

SOURCES

BIBLIOGRAPHY

INDEX

ABOUT THE AUTHOR

George F. Gruner, a native Californian, retired in 1988 after a career in journalism covering forty-six years, including thirty-three years with *The Fresno Bee*. Born in Alameda in 1925, he joined the news staff of the *Oakland Tribune* in the hectic early months of World War II and, following military service, returned there after the war. He later spent two years on the civilian staff of *The Stars and Stripes*, the armed forces newspaper in Europe. At *The Bee*, his last assignment was as executive editor — he was the chief news executive for seventeen years. On his

retirement, McClatchy Newspapers established the George F. Gruner Awards, presented annually by the Journalism Department of California State University, Fresno, to recognize meritorious public service journalism in Central California.

Gruner also is the author of *Blue Water Beat: The Two Lives Of the Battleship USS* California, a definitive history of BB-44, the only modern battleship ever built on the Pacific Coast, also published by the Associates of the National Maritime Museum Library (Glencannon Press, 1996). His interest in the White Flyers began in childhood — he retains vivid pierside memories of a gala departure of the *Yale* from San Francisco back in the Thirties. Those memories led to his resolve to bring the *Yale* and her sister, the *Harvard,* back through the mists of time.

Ironically, maritime historian Gruner is a World War II Army veteran, having served with an anti-aircraft artillery unit in France, Belgium, Holland and Germany, including the Battle of the Bulge. His most vivid memories of the sea include a smooth and speedy five-day Atlantic crossing with 15,000 other GIs on the then-troopship *Queen Elizabeth*; his fifteen-day return home in the hold of a tossing Liberty Ship in a stormy North Atlantic winter; forty-seven glorious postwar days in the confines of a small Dutch freighter steaming from Oakland to London, and the gut-wrenching jolt of a tailhook landing on the aircraft carrier USS *Constellation* (CV-64), capped by the back blast of a full sixteen-inch-gun broadside aboard the battleship USS *New Jersey* (BB-62). His last sea experience was a six-day trip up the Pacific Coast, one of the final voyages of the nuclear cruiser USS *California* (CGN-36) before she, too, went to the scrapheap.

Sources

Most of the information in this history of two great ships is based on contemporary reports in newspapers and other journals in Atlantic and Pacific port cities. When significant quotations are used, the source is identified in the text.

Famous American Ships by maritime historian Frank O. Braynard (Hastings House), served as the impetus for this work by offering just enough information about the *Yale* and *Harvard* to make the writer want to know more. A complete history of Pacific Coast passenger lines is contained in *Ships That Sail No More,* by Giles T. Brown (University of Kentucky Press). Brown also wrote *The Admiral Line and Its Competitors: the Zenith and Decline Of Shipping Along the Pacific Coast*, a doctoral dissertation at Claremont-McKenna College, Claremont, California.

Brown's works blended with *History of the Los Angeles Steamship Co.*, a master's thesis by James M. Merrill, at the Claremont Graduate School. Both were students of Professor John Haskell Kemble, a historian of national stature and author of many books and articles on maritime subjects. His papers in Claremont's Honnold/Mudd Library and in The Huntington Library in San Marino included much valuable information from shipping-line documents and photographs (All items credited to the Huntington Library are reproduced by permission).

Technical details about the two ships and the construction period in Chester, Pennsylvania and Hoboken, New Jersey, were provided in two issues (February 7 and August 8, 1907) of a New York publication, *The Nautical Gazette*, which billed itself as "An Illustrated Weekly Journal of Navigation, Shipbuilding, Marine Engineering, Naval Architecture and Commerce." Photographs of the hull and interiors were of a quality exceeded only by the detail in the text.

Background on Charles W. Morse came from the *Dictionary of American Biography,* Volume VII, edited by Dumas Malone (Charles Scribners Sons). His difficulties with contemporary business tycoons are presented in *A Productive Monopoly: The Effect of Railroad Control on New England Coastal Steamship Lines, 1870-1916* by William Leonhard Taylor (Brown University Press). Additional information is provided in *The Era of the Joy Line — A Saga of Steamboating on Long Island Sound* by Edwin L. Dunbaugh (Greenwood Press). Dr. Dunbaugh, a professor of history at Hofstra University, also is a co-author of *Eastern Steamship* which provided much information about the fast turbiners' early years in the Atlantic. He completed the work started by the late David Crockett, president of the Steamship Historical Society of America, and published by the society.

Sketchy records of the fast turbiners' service in the U.S. Navy in World War I (and the *Yale* in World War II) are to be found in the National Archives in Washington. Record Group 24, General Records, Logs of Ships and Stations, 1801-1946, provides some information on operations of the *Yale* and the *Charles* in the English Channel. Beyond a sentence or two, no logs could be found of the *Greyhound.* Some details concerning the ship's Alaskan operations were found in the National Archives Regional Repository in Seattle, in logs of the Puget Sound Navy Yard and in Record Group 181, Ship File, USS *Greyhound.* More complete are the files in the Ships Histories Branch in the Naval Historical Center at the Washington Navy Yard, Anacostia. The *Dictionary of American Naval Fighting Ships*, published by the Naval History Division, Department of the Navy, provides basic information on each ship's service career.

The Archives in Washington also is the repository of records relating to the loss of the *Harvard* at Point Arguello, California, in 1931. Record Group 41, Records of the Bureau of Marine Inspection and Navigation, Steamboat Inspection Service, Annual Report of Accidents Investigated, 1911-37, gives details of the grounding and the penalties applied to the *Harvard*'s officers. Record Group 80, Secretary of the Navy General

Correspondence, 1926-40, contains the report of the officer in charge of the Point Arguello Radio Direction Finder station and the details of the rescue of the liner's passengers as set forth by the captain of the new cruiser USS *Louisville*. The Navy's previous involvement with Point Arguello is detailed in *Tragedy at Honda*, by Vice Adm. (Ret.) Charles A. Lockwood and Col. (Ret. USAF) Hans Christian Adamson (Valley Publishers).

BIBLIOGRAPHY

Books:

Albion, Robert G. *Five Centuries of Famous Ships*. New York: McGraw-Hill Book Company, 1978.

Braynard, Frank O. *Famous American Ships*. New York: Hastings House Publishers, 1956, 1978.

Brown, Giles T. *Ships That Sail No More: Marine Transportation from San Diego to Puget Sound, 1910-1940.*" Lexington: University of Kentucky Press, 1966.

Crockett, David, and Dunbaugh, Edwin L. *Eastern Steamship*. Providence, R.I.: Steamship Historical Society of America, 1997.

Dunbaugh, Edwin L. *The Era of the Joy Line: A Saga of Steamboating on Long Island Sound*. Westport, Conn.: Greenwood Press, 1982.

Emmons, Frederick E. *American Passenger Ships: The Ocean Lines and Liners*. Newark: University of Delaware Press, 1985.

Hice, Charles. *The Last Hours of Seven Four Stackers*. Miamisburg, Ohio: The Ohioan Company, 1967.

Lockwood, Vice Adm. (ret.) Charles A., and Adamson, Col. (ret. USAF) Hans Christian, *Tragedy at Honda*. Fresno: Valley Publishers, 1960.

Lott, Lt. Cmdr. Arnold C. *A Long Line of Ships: Mare Island's Century of Naval Activity in California*. Annapolis: U.S. Naval Institute Press, 1954.

MacMullen, Jerry. *They Came By Sea: A Pictorial History of San Diego Bay*. San Diego: The Ward Ritchie Press and the Maritime Museum Association of San Diego, 1969.

Malone, Dumas, editor. *Dictionary of American Biography*, Vol. VII. New York: Charles Scribner's Sons, 1934.

Miller, Robert. *The New York Coastwise Trade (1865-1915)*. New York: Library Editions Ltd., 1970.

Niven, John. *The American President Lines and Its Forebears, 1848-1984*. Newark: University of Delaware Press.

Taylor, William Leonhard. *A Productive Monopoly: The Effect of Railroad Control on New England Coastal Steamship Lines, 1870-1916*. Providence, R.I.: Brown University Press.

Dictionary of American Naval Fighting Ships. Washington: Navy Department, Office of Chief of Naval Operations, Naval History Division.

Doctoral Dissertation:

Brown, Giles T. *The Admiral Line and Its Competitors: the Zenith and Decline Of Shipping Along the Pacific Coast*. Claremont, Calif.: Claremont-McKenna College

Master's Thesis:

Merrill, James M. *History of the Los Angeles Steamship Co*. Claremont, Calif.: Claremont Graduate School.

Articles:

Gardner, J. Howland. "The Development of Steam Navigation on Long Island Sound." *Transactions of the Society of Naval Architects and Marine Engineers, 1893-1943*, reprinted 1994 by the Steamship Historical Society of America.

Hadaway, Lt. Cmdr. (USNR) Richard B. "Course Zero Nine Five." Annapolis, MD: *U.S. Naval Institute Proceedings*, January, 1957.

Heffernan, John Paul. "Charles W. Morse: Bath's King of Ice and Steam." *Down East, The Magazine of Maine*, January, 1976.

Johnson, Capt. John. "The Wreck of the Harvard." *Steamboat Bill*, publication of the Steamboat Historical Society of America, Winter, 1960.

Mueller, Edward A. "The Merchants and Miners Transportation Company." *Steamboat Bill*, Summer, 1990.

Roberts, Glenn O. "The Admiral Line: A Short History of the Pacific Steamship Company." *Steamboat Bill*, December, 1957.

Stone, P.M. "The Boston-New York Passenger Service, 1907-1941." Outline chronology in *Steamboat Bill*, June, 1954.

Wagner, Jack. "Destruction Stalked the Twins." *Westward* magazine, published by Kaiser Steel Company; September, 1954.

"The Ill-Fated Harvard." *Westways* magazine, March, 1938.

"Fiftieth Anniversary of the Old Roach Yard." *The Chester Compass*, employee publication of the Merchant Shipbuilding Corporation, June, 1921.

"Launch of the American Turbine Steamship Yale." New York: *The Nautical Gazette*, Illustrated Weekly Journal of Navigation, Shipbuilding, Marine Engineering, Naval Architecture and Commerce, Dec. 29, 1906.

"Launch of the New American Turbine Steamship Harvard." *The Nautical Gazette*, Feb. 7, 1907.

"New American Turbine Steamers Yale and Harvard." *The Nautical Gazette*, Aug. 8, 1907.

"T.S.S. Yale Goes Over the Hill." *Pacific Marine Review*, August, 1949.

Newspapers:

Bath, Maine, *Herald*
Los Angeles Examiner
Los Angeles Evening Herald
Los Angeles Times
Marine Digest, Seattle, Wash.
New York Times
San Diego Sun
San Diego Union
San Francisco Call-Bulletin
San Francisco Chronicle
San Francisco Examiner
San Francisco News

Index

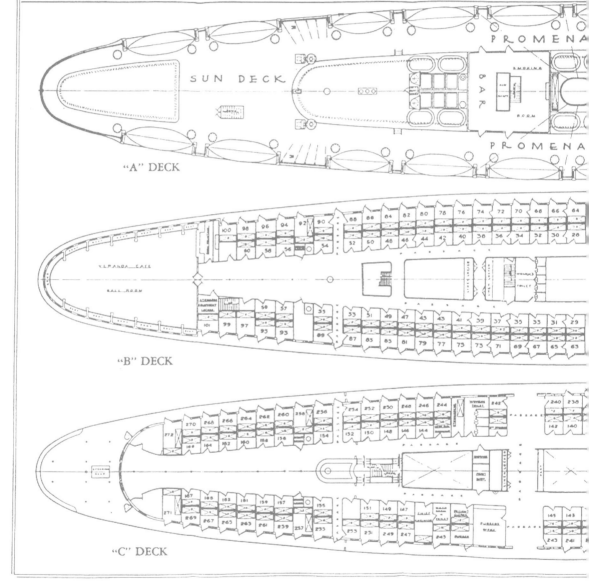

LOS ANGELES STEAMSHIP COMPANY'S
23 - KNOT SUPER - EXPRESS STEAMER

S. S

"A" DECK

"B" DECK

"C" DECK